Table of Contents

Preface...ix

Reading Schedule...xiii

Pronunciation Guide.. xvi

Pattern Letters... xviii

Sight (Memorization) Word Cards... xx

2 Nephi...1

Jacob..30

Enos..65

Jarom..70

Omni...74

Words of Mormon...79

Mosiah..83

Endnotes and Sources Consulted...214

Reading Schedule

Reading Assignment	Day	Personal Check-off	Reading Assignment	Day	Personal Check-off
2 Nephi 26:1–1–5	248		Jacob 2:1–6	284	
2 Nephi 26:6–9	249		Jacob 2:7–10	285	
2 Nephi 26:10–14	250		Jacob 2:11–15	286	
2 Nephi 26:15–18	251		Jacob 2:16–22	287	
2 Nephi 26:19–24	252		Jacob 2:23–29	288	
2 Nephi 26:25–30	253		Jacob 2:30–35	289	
2 Nephi 26:31–33	254		Jacob 3:1–5	290	
2 Nephi 27:1–5	255		Jacob 3:6–9	291	
2 Nephi 27:6–10	256		Jacob 3:10–14	292	
2 Nephi 27:11–15	257		Jacob 4:1–4	293	
2 Nephi 27:16–22	258		Jacob 4:5–8	294	
2 Nephi 27:23–27	259		Jacob 4:9–13	295	
2 Nephi 27:28–35	260		Jacob 4:14–18	296	
2 Nephi 28:1–6	261		Jacob 5:1–6	297	
2 Nephi 28:7–12	262		Jacob 5:7–11	298	
2 Nephi 28:13–18	263		Jacob 5:12–17	299	
2 Nephi 28:19–25	264		Jacob 5:18–21	300	
2 Nephi 28:26–32	265		Jacob 5:22–26	301	
2 Nephi 29:1–4	266		Jacob 5:27–31	302	
2 Nephi 29:5–8	267		Jacob 5:32–37	303	
2 Nephi 29:9–14	268		Jacob 5:38–43	304	
2 Nephi 30:1–5	269		Jacob 5:44–47	305	
2 Nephi 30:6–11	270		Jacob 5:48–53	306	
2 Nephi 30:12–18	271		Jacob 5:54–59	307	
2 Nephi 31:1–6	272		Jacob 5:60–64	308	
2 Nephi 31:7–12	273		Jacob 5:65–70	309	
2 Nephi 31:13–16	274		Jacob 5:71–74	310	
2 Nephi 31:17–21	275		Jacob 5:75–77	311	
2 Nephi 32:1–5	276		Jacob 6:1–6	312	
2 Nephi 32:6–9	277		Jacob 6:7–13	313	
2 Nephi 33:1–5	278		Jacob 7:1–5	314	
2 Nephi 33:6–10	279		Jacob 7:6–11	315	
2 Nephi 33:11–15	280		Jacob 7:12–17	316	
Jacob 1:1–5	281		Jacob 7:18–23	317	
Jacob 1:6–10	282		Jacob 7:24–27	318	
Jacob 1:11–19	283		Enos 1:1–6	319	

Reading Schedule

Reading Assignment	Day	Personal Check-off	Reading Assignment	Day	Personal Check-off
Enos 1:7–12	320		Mosiah 4:9–13	356	
Enos 1:13–17	321		Mosiah 4:14–18	357	
Enos 1:18–22	322		Mosiah 4:19–23	358	
Enos 1:23–27	323		Mosiah 4:24–27	359	
Jarom 1:1–4	324		Mosiah 4:28–30	360	
Jarom 1:5–9	325		Mosiah 5:1–5	361	
Jarom 1:10–15	326		Mosiah 5:6–9	362	
Omni 1:1–5	327		Mosiah 5:10–15	363	
Omni 1:6–10	328		Mosiah 6:1–7	364	
Omni 1:11–14	329		Mosiah 7:1–7	365	
Omni 1:15–19	330		Mosiah 7:8–12	366	
Omni 1:20–25	331		Mosiah 7:13–16	367	
Omni 1:26–30	332		Mosiah 7:17–20	368	
Words of Mormon 1:1–4	333		Mosiah 7:21–25	369	
Words of Mormon 1:5–9	334		Mosiah 7:26–33	370	
Words of Mormon 1:10–13	335		Mosiah 8:1–6	371	
Words of Mormon 1:14–18	336		Mosiah 8:7–11	372	
Mosiah 1:1–4	337		Mosiah 8:12–16	373	
Mosiah 1:5–8	338		Mosiah 8:17–21	374	
Mosiah 1:9–13	339		Mosiah 9:1–4	375	
Mosiah 1:14–18	340		Mosiah 9:5–10	376	
Mosiah 2:1–5	341		Mosiah 9:11–14	377	
Mosiah 2:6–9	342		Mosiah 9:15–19	378	
Mosiah 2:10–14	343		Mosiah 10:1–5	379	
Mosiah 2:15–20	344		Mosiah 10:6–10	380	
Mosiah 2:21–26	345		Mosiah 10:11–15	381	
Mosiah 2:27–30	346		Mosiah 10:16–22	382	
Mosiah 2:31–35	347		Mosiah 11:1–5	383	
Mosiah 2:36–40	348		Mosiah 11:6–11	384	
Mosiah 3:1–6	349		Mosiah 11:12–16	385	
Mosiah 3:7–11	350		Mosiah 11:17–22	386	
Mosiah 3:12–17	351		Mosiah 11:23–29	387	
Mosiah 3:18–21	352		Mosiah 12:1–4	388	
Mosiah 3:22–27	353		Mosiah 12:5–10	389	
Mosiah 4:1–4	354		Mosiah 12:11–16	390	
Mosiah 4:5–8	355		Mosiah 12:17–24	391	

Reading Schedule

Reading Assignment	Day	Personal Check-off	Reading Assignment	Day	Personal Check-off
Mosiah 12:25–29	392		Mosiah 21:26–30	429	
Mosiah 12:30–37	393		Mosiah 21:31–36	430	
Mosiah 13:1–6	394		Mosiah 22:1–5	431	
Mosiah 13:7–14	395		Mosiah 22:6–11	432	
Mosiah 13:15–25	396		Mosiah 22:12–16	434	
Mosiah 13:26–31	397		Mosiah 23:1–8	435	
Mosiah 13:32–35	398		Mosiah 23:9–15	436	
Mosiah 14:1–6	399		Mosiah 23:16–24	437	
Mosiah 14:7–12	400		Mosiah 23:25–31	438	
Mosiah 15:1–7	401		Mosiah 23:32–39	439	
Mosiah 15:8–12	402		Mosiah 24:1–6	440	
Mosiah 15:13–19	403		Mosiah 24:7–11	441	
Mosiah 15:20–25	404		Mosiah 24:12–18	442	
Mosiah 15:26–31	405		Mosiah 24:19–25	443	
Mosiah 16:1–6	406		Mosiah 25:1–8	444	
Mosiah 16:7–15	407		Mosiah 25:9–13	445	
Mosiah 17:1–7	408		Mosiah 25:14–18	446	
Mosiah 17:8–13	409		Mosiah 25:19–24	447	
Mosiah 17:14–20	410		Mosiah 26:1–7	448	
Mosiah 18:1–6	411		Mosiah 26:8–13	449	
Mosiah 18:7–11	412		Mosiah 26:14–22	450	
Mosiah 18:12–16	413		Mosiah 26:23–29	451	
Mosiah 18:17–22	414		Mosiah 26:30–39	452	
Mosiah 18:23–28	415		Mosiah 27:1–5	453	
Mosiah 18:29–35	416		Mosiah 27:6–10	454	
Mosiah 19:1–8	417		Mosiah 27:11–15	455	
Mosiah 19:9–14	418		Mosiah 27:16–21	456	
Mosiah 19:15–21	419		Mosiah 27:22–27	457	
Mosiah 19:22–29	420		Mosiah 27:28–31	458	
Mosiah 20:1–6	421		Mosiah 27:32–37	459	
Mosiah 20:7–12	422		Mosiah 28:1–4	460	
Mosiah 20:13–18	423		Mosiah 28:5–11	461	
Mosiah 20:19–26	424		Mosiah 28:12–16	462	
Mosiah 21:1–7	425		Mosiah 28:17–20	463	
Mosiah 21:8–14	426		Mosiah 29:1–7	464	
Mosiah 21:15–20	427		Mosiah 29:8–13	465	
Mosiah 21:21–25	428		Mosiah 29:14–20	466	

Pronunciation Guide

Symbol Key

a, e, i, o, u *(lower case)*—Short vowels

A, E, I, O, U *(upper case)*—Long vowels

R *(uppercase)*—Consonant names

ə *(Schwa)*—Translates to "uh" sound, see Alma 20

/ou/—Abnormal sound *(house)*

/ow/—Abnormal sound *(now)*

/oi/—Abnormal sound *(join)*

/oy/—Abnormal sound *(joy)*

/ŏŏ/—Abnormal sound *(good)*

Note: all consonant blends will be noted by slashes (example: /sh/)

Similar Letters and Sounds

Symbol	Example
Short A	
a	apple
Short E	
e	bed
Short I	
i	pin
Short O	
o	hot
al	talk
au	haul
aw	saw
Short U	
u	rug
Long A	
A	cake
ai	paid
ay	way
ei	their
ey	they
Long E	
E	these
ee	feed
ea	speak

Symbol	Example
Long I	
I	kite
ie	pie
igh	high
y	by
ye	bye
Long O	
O	hope
oa	oath
ow	grow
Long U	
ue	True
ui	ruin
ew	drew
oo	food
Abnormal sounds	
/ŏŏ/	good
/ou/	house
/ow/	now
/oi/	join
/oy/	toy

Note: see the Pronunciation Guide in the Book of Mormon for names of people and places.

2 Nephi 27

1 But, behold, in the last days, or in the days of the Gentiles—yea, behold all the nations of the Gentiles and also the Jews, both those who shall come upon this land and those who shall be upon other lands, yea, even upon all the lands of the earth, behold, they will be drunken with iniquity and all manner of abominations—

2 And when that day shall come they shall be visited of the Lord of Hosts, with thunder and with earthquake, and with a great noise, and with storm, and with tempest, and with the flame of devouring fire.

3 And all the nations that fight against Zion, and that distress her, shall be as a dream of a night vision; yea, it shall be unto them, even as unto a hungry man which dreameth, and behold he eateth but he awaketh and his soul is empty; or like unto a thirsty man which dreameth, and behold he drinketh but he awaketh and behold he is faint, and his soul hath appetite; yea, even so shall the multitude of all the nations be that fight against Mount Zion.

4 For behold, all ye that doeth iniquity, stay yourselves and wonder, for ye shall cry out, and cry; yea, ye shall be drunken but not with wine, ye shall stagger but not with strong drink.

5 For behold, the Lord hath poured out upon you the spirit of deep sleep. For behold, ye have closed your eyes, and ye have rejected the prophets; and your rulers, and the seers hath he covered because of your iniquity.

Date _____
☐ Completed

6 And it shall come to pass that the Lord God shall bring forth unto you the words of a book, and they shall be the words of them which have slumbered.

7 And behold the book shall be sealed; and in the book shall be a revelation from God, from the beginning of the world to the ending thereof.

8 Wherefore, because of the things which are sealed up, the things which are sealed shall not be delivered in the day of the wickedness and abominations of the people. Wherefore the book shall be kept from them.

9 But the book shall be delivered unto a man, and he shall deliver the words of the book, which are the words of those who have slumbered in the dust, and he shall deliver these words unto another;

10 But the words which are sealed he shall not deliver, neither shall he deliver the book. For the book shall be sealed by the power of God, and the revelation which was sealed shall be kept in the book until the own due time of the Lord, that they may come forth; for behold, they reveal all things from the foundation of the world unto the end thereof.

Date _____
☐ Completed

11 And the day cometh that the words of the book which were sealed shall be read upon the house tops; and they shall be read by the power of

Christ; and all things shall be revealed unto the children of men which ever have been among the children of men, and which ever will be even unto the end of the earth.

12 Wherefore, at that day when the book shall be delivered unto the man of whom I have spoken, the book shall be hid from the eyes of the world, that the eyes of none shall behold it save it be that three witnesses shall behold it, by the power of God, besides him to whom the book shall be delivered; and they shall testify to the truth of the book and the things therein.

13 And there is none other which shall view it, save it be a few according to the will of God, to bear testimony of his word unto the children of men; for the Lord God hath said that the words of the faithful should speak as if it were from the dead.

14 Wherefore, the Lord God will proceed to bring forth the words of the book; and in the mouth of as many witnesses as seemeth him good will he establish his word; and wo be unto him that rejecteth the word of God!

15 But behold, it shall come to pass that the Lord God shall say unto him to whom he shall deliver the book: Take these words which are not sealed and deliver them to another, that he may show them unto the learned, saying: Read this, I pray thee. And the learned shall say: Bring hither the book, and I will read them.

16 And now, because of the glory of the world and to get gain will they say this, and not for the glory of God.

17 And the man shall say: I cannot bring the book, for it is sealed.

18 Then shall the learned say: I cannot read it.

19 Wherefore it shall come to pass, that the Lord God will deliver again the book and the words thereof to him that is not learned; and the man that is not learned shall say: I am not learned.

20 Then shall the Lord God say unto him: The learned shall not read them, for they have rejected them, and I am able to do mine own work; wherefore thou shalt read the words which I shall give unto thee.

21 Touch not the things which are sealed, for I will bring them forth in mine own due time; for I will show unto the children of men that I am able to do mine own work.

22 Wherefore, when thou hast read the words which I have commanded thee, and obtained the witnesses which I have promised unto thee, then shalt thou seal up the book again, and hide it up unto me, that I may preserve the words which thou hast not read, until I shall see fit in mine own wisdom to reveal all things unto the children of men.

23 For behold, I am God; and I am a God of miracles; and I will show unto the world that I am the same yesterday, today, and forever; and I

Date _____
☐ Completed

Date _____
☐ Completed

work not among the children of men save it be according to their faith.

24 And again it shall come to pass that the Lord shall say unto him that shall read the words that shall be delivered him:

25 Forasmuch as this people draw near unto me with their mouth, and with their lips do honor me, but have removed their hearts far from me, and their fear towards me is taught by the precepts of men—

26 Therefore, I will proceed to do a marvelous work among this people, yea, a marvelous work and a wonder, for the wisdom of their wise and learned shall perish, and the understanding of their prudent shall be hid.

27 And wo unto them that seek deep to hide their counsel from the Lord! And their works are in the dark; and they say: Who seeth us, and who knoweth us? And they also say: Surely, your turning of things upside down shall be esteemed as the potter's clay. But behold, I will show unto them, saith the Lord of Hosts, that I know all their works. For shall the work say of him that made it, he made me not? Or shall the thing framed say of him that framed it, he had no understanding?

28 But behold, saith the Lord of Hosts: I will show unto the children of men that it is yet a very little while and Lebanon shall be turned into a fruitful field; and the fruitful field shall be esteemed as a forest.

29 And in that day shall the deaf hear the words of the book, and the eyes of the blind shall see out of obscurity and out of darkness.

30 And the meek also shall increase, and their joy shall be in the Lord, and the poor among men shall rejoice in the Holy One of Israel.

31 For assuredly as the Lord liveth they shall see that the terrible one is brought to naught, and the scorner is consumed, and all that watch for iniquity are cut off;

32 And they that make a man an offender for a word, and lay a snare for him that reproveth in the gate, and turn aside the just for a thing of naught.

33 Therefore, thus saith the Lord, who redeemed Abraham, concerning the house of Jacob: Jacob shall not now be ashamed, neither shall his face now wax pale.

34 But when he seeth his children, the work of my hands, in the midst of him, they shall sanctify my name, and sanctify the Holy One of Jacob, and shall fear the God of Israel.

35 They also that erred in spirit shall come to understanding, and they that murmured shall learn doctrine.

Notes

Date _____
☐ Completed

Date _____
☐ Completed

5

2 Nephi

Chapter 28

Sight (Memorization) Words

death

Pattern Word

Pattern word	-age
Key words in scriptures	**rage**
Location in chapter	Verse 20
Other words made from this pattern not found in chapter	age, cage, gage, page, wage, stage

Phonics Application

- *Long Vowel Sounds:* the long sound of vowels make the sound of the letter.
  - The long sound of A (example: **a**te)
- *The Silent E rule:* when an E is at the end of a word, the E is silent and it makes the vowel to the left say its name. (When other rules apply to the word, a word that ends in E is still silent, for example: serve [see R-Controlled Vowels].)
- *Consonant-Vowel-Blend and Blend-Vowel-Blend:* these patterns are the merging together of sounds to make words. A blend is the combination of two (or more) consonants together. These are the blends: BL, CL, FL, GL, PL, SL, BR, CR, DR, FR, GR, PR, TR, SC, SK, SM, SN, SP, ST, SW, TW.
- *Consonant Diagraphs:* diagraphs are two letters that make one sound. The diagraphs are TH, CH, SH, WH.
- *Complex Consonants:* blends that include three consonants, two consonants that sounds like a single letter, and consonant and vowel clusters. The complex consonants are QU, TCH, CK.

Recommended (Age Appropriate) Reading Chunks

- Verses 1–6
- Verses 7–12
- Verses 13–18
- Verses 19–25
- Verses 26–32

Gospel Principle Review/Activity

- What is apostasy and how can you see it today?
- How will we know which church is the Lord's true church?
- What will happen to those who teach the wrong things?
- *Activity:* The Lord tries to teach us that it is better to build on a rock than on a sandy foundation.
  - Take some items to build a small toy house and go outside to find sand/dirt and concrete/rock (try to make the house firm for both places).
  - What happens to the house when a river of water comes?
  - If you sprinkle water, what happens?
  - What is the Lord trying to teach us?

Word Patterns

_age

Words made with –age word pattern.
Use alphabet letters to create words.

2 Nephi 28

1 And now, behold, my brethren, I have spoken unto you, according as the Spirit hath constrained me; wherefore, I know that they must surely come to pass.

2 And the things which shall be written out of the book shall be of great worth unto the children of men, and especially unto our seed, which is a remnant of the house of Israel.

3 For it shall come to pass in that day that the churches which are built up, and not unto the Lord, when the one shall say unto the other: Behold, I, I am the Lord's; and the others shall say: I, I am the Lord's; and thus shall every one say that hath built up churches, and not unto the Lord—

4 And they shall contend one with another; and their priests shall contend one with another, and they shall teach with their learning, and deny the Holy Ghost, which giveth utterance.

5 And they deny the power of God, the Holy One of Israel; and they say unto the people: Hearken unto us, and hear ye our precept; for behold there is no God today, for the Lord and the Redeemer hath done his work, and he hath given his power unto men;

6 Behold, hearken ye unto my precept; if they shall say there is a miracle wrought by the hand of the Lord, believe it not; for this day he is not a God of miracles; he hath done his work.

Date _____

☐ Completed

7 Yea, and there shall be many which shall say: Eat, drink, and be merry, for tomorrow we die; and it shall be well with us.

8 And there shall also be many which shall say: Eat, drink, and be merry; nevertheless, fear God—he will justify in committing a little sin; yea, lie a little, take the advantage of one because of his words, dig a pit for thy neighbor; there is no harm in this; and do all these things, for tomorrow we die; and if it so be that we are guilty, God will beat us with a few stripes, and at last we shall be saved in the kingdom of God.

9 Yea, and there shall be many which shall teach after this manner, false and vain and foolish doctrines, and shall be puffed up in their hearts, and shall seek deep to hide their counsels from the Lord; and their works shall be in the dark.

10 And the blood of the saints shall cry from the ground against them.

11 Yea, they have all gone out of the way; they have become corrupted.

12 Because of pride, and because of false teachers, and false doctrine, their churches have become corrupted, and their churches are lifted up; because of pride they are puffed up.

13 They rob the poor because of their fine sanctuaries; they rob the poor because of their fine clothing; and they persecute the meek and the poor in heart, because in their pride they are puffed up.

14 They wear stiff necks and high heads; yea, and because of pride, and wickedness, and abominations, and whoredoms, they have all gone astray save it be a few, who are the humble followers of Christ; nevertheless, they are led, that in many instances they do err because they are taught by the precepts of men.

15 O the wise, and the learned, and the rich, that are puffed up in the pride of their hearts, and all those who preach false doctrines, and all those who commit whoredoms, and pervert the right way of the Lord, wo, wo, wo be unto them, saith the Lord God Almighty, for they shall be thrust down to hell!

16 Wo unto them that turn aside the just for a thing of naught and revile against that which is good, and say that it is of no worth! For the day shall come that the Lord God will speedily visit the inhabitants of the earth; and in that day that they are fully ripe in iniquity they shall perish.

17 But behold, if the inhabitants of the earth shall repent of their wickedness and abominations they shall not be destroyed, saith the Lord of Hosts.

18 But behold, that great and abominable church, the whore of all the earth, must tumble to the earth, and great must be the fall thereof.

19 For the kingdom of the devil must shake, and they which belong to it must needs be stirred up unto repentance, or the devil will grasp them with his everlasting chains, and they be stirred up to anger, and perish;

20 For behold, at that day shall he rage in the hearts of the children of men, and stir them up to anger against that which is good.

21 And others will he pacify, and lull them away into carnal security, that they will say: All is well in Zion; yea, Zion prospereth, all is well—and thus the devil cheateth their souls, and leadeth them away carefully down to hell.

22 And behold, others he flattereth away, and telleth them there is no hell; and he saith unto them: I am no devil, for there is none—and thus he whispereth in their ears, until he grasps them with his awful chains, from whence there is no deliverance.

23 Yea, they are grasped with death, and hell; and death, and hell, and the devil, and all that have been seized therewith must stand before the throne of God, and be judged according to their works, from whence they must go into the place prepared for them, even a lake of fire and brimstone, which is endless torment.

24 Therefore, wo be unto him that is at ease in Zion!

25 Wo be unto him that crieth: All is well!

26 Yea, wo be unto him that hearkeneth unto the precepts of men, and denieth the power of God, and the gift of the Holy Ghost!

27 Yea, wo be unto him that saith: We have received, and we need no more!

Date _____
☐ Completed

Date _____
☐ Completed

28 And in fine, wo unto all those who tremble, and are angry because of the truth of God! For behold, he that is built upon the rock receiveth it with gladness; and he that is built upon a sandy foundation trembleth lest he shall fall.

29 Wo be unto him that shall say: We have received the word of God, and we need no more of the word of God, for we have enough!

30 For behold, thus saith the Lord God: I will give unto the children of men line upon line, precept upon precept, here a little and there a little; and blessed are those who hearken unto my precepts, and lend an ear unto my counsel, for they shall learn wisdom; for unto him that receiveth I will give more; and from them that shall say, We have enough, from them shall be taken away even that which they have.

31 Cursed is he that putteth his trust in man, or maketh flesh his arm, or shall hearken unto the precepts of men, save their precepts shall be given by the power of the Holy Ghost.

32 Wo be unto the Gentiles, saith the Lord God of Hosts! For notwithstanding I shall lengthen out mine arm unto them from day to day, they will deny me; nevertheless, I will be merciful unto them, saith the Lord God, if they will repent and come unto me; for mine arm is lengthened out all the day long, saith the Lord God of Hosts.

Notes

Date _____

☐ Completed

2 Nephi 29

1 But behold, there shall be many—at that day when I shall proceed to do a marvelous work among them, that I may remember my covenants which I have made unto the children of men, that I may set my hand again the second time to recover my people, which are of the house of Israel;

2 And also, that I may remember the promises which I have made unto thee, Nephi, and also unto thy father, that I would remember your seed; and that the words of your seed should proceed forth out of my mouth unto your seed; and my words shall hiss forth unto the ends of the earth, for a standard unto my people, which are of the house of Israel;

3 And because my words shall hiss forth—many of the Gentiles shall say: A Bible! A Bible! We have got a Bible, and there cannot be any more Bible.

4 But thus saith the Lord God: O fools, they shall have a Bible; and it shall proceed forth from the Jews, mine ancient covenant people. And what thank they the Jews for the Bible which they receive from them? Yea, what do the Gentiles mean? Do they remember the travails, and the labors, and the pains of the Jews, and their diligence unto me, in bringing forth salvation unto the Gentiles?

5 O ye Gentiles, have ye remembered the Jews, mine ancient covenant people? Nay; but ye have cursed them, and have hated them, and have not sought to recover them. But behold, I will return all these things upon your own heads; for I the Lord have not forgotten my people.

6 Thou fool, that shall say: A Bible, we have got a Bible, and we need no more Bible. Have ye obtained a Bible save it were by the Jews?

7 Know ye not that there are more nations than one? Know ye not that I, the Lord your God, have created all men, and that I remember those who are upon the isles of the sea; and that I rule in the heavens above and in the earth beneath; and I bring forth my word unto the children of men, yea, even upon all the nations of the earth?

8 Wherefore murmur ye, because that ye shall receive more of my word? Know ye not that the testimony of two nations is a witness unto you that I am God, that I remember one nation like unto another? Wherefore, I speak the same words unto one nation like unto another. And when the two nations shall run together the testimony of the two nations shall run together also.

9 And I do this that I may prove unto many that I am the same yesterday, today, and forever; and that I speak forth my words according to mine own pleasure. And because that I have spoken one word ye need

Date _____
☐ Completed

Date _____
☐ Completed

not suppose that I cannot speak another; for my work is not yet finished; neither shall it be until the end of man, neither from that time henceforth and forever.

10 Wherefore, because that ye have a Bible ye need not suppose that it contains all my words; neither need ye suppose that I have not caused more to be written.

11 For I command all men, both in the east and in the west, and in the north, and in the south, and in the islands of the sea, that they shall write the words which I speak unto them; for out of the books which shall be written I will judge the world, every man according to their works, according to that which is written.

12 For behold, I shall speak unto the Jews and they shall write it; and I shall also speak unto the Nephites and they shall write it; and I shall also speak unto the other tribes of the house of Israel, which I have led away, and they shall write it; and I shall also speak unto all nations of the earth and they shall write it.

13 And it shall come to pass that the Jews shall have the words of the Nephites, and the Nephites shall have the words of the Jews; and the Nephites and the Jews shall have the words of the lost tribes of Israel; and the lost tribes of Israel shall have the words of the Nephites and the Jews.

14 And it shall come to pass that my people, which are of the house of Israel, shall be gathered home unto the lands of their possessions; and my word also shall be gathered in one. And I will show unto them that fight against my word and against my people, who are of the house of Israel, that I am God, and that I covenanted with Abraham that I would remember his seed forever.

2 Nephi 30

1 And now behold, my beloved brethren, I would speak unto you; for I, Nephi, would not suffer that ye should suppose that ye are more righteous than the Gentiles shall be. For behold, except ye shall keep the commandments of God ye shall all likewise perish; and because of the words which have been spoken ye need not suppose that the Gentiles are utterly destroyed.

2 For behold, I say unto you that as many of the Gentiles as will repent are the covenant people of the Lord; and as many of the Jews as will not repent shall be cast off; for the Lord covenanteth with none save it be with them that repent and believe in his Son, who is the Holy One of Israel.

3 And now, I would prophesy somewhat more concerning the Jews and the Gentiles. For after the book of which I have spoken shall come forth, and be written unto the Gentiles, and sealed up again unto the Lord, there shall be many which shall believe the words which are written; and they shall carry them forth unto the remnant of our seed.

4 And then shall the remnant of our seed know concerning us, how that we came out from Jerusalem, and that they are descendants of the Jews.

5 And the gospel of Jesus Christ shall be declared among them; wherefore, they shall be restored unto the knowledge of their fathers, and also to the knowledge of Jesus Christ, which was had among their fathers.

Date _____

☐ Completed

6 And then shall they rejoice; for they shall know that it is a blessing unto them from the hand of God; and their scales of darkness shall begin to fall from their eyes; and many generations shall not pass away among them, save they shall be a pure and a delightsome people.

7 And it shall come to pass that the Jews which are scattered also shall begin to believe in Christ; and they shall begin to gather in upon the face of the land; and as many as shall believe in Christ shall also become a delightsome people.

8 And it shall come to pass that the Lord God shall commence his work among all nations, kindreds, tongues, and people, to bring about the restoration of his people upon the earth.

9 And with righteousness shall the Lord God judge the poor, and reprove with equity for the meek of the earth. And he shall smite the earth with the rod of his mouth; and with the breath of his lips shall he slay the wicked.

10 For the time speedily cometh that the Lord God shall cause a great division among the people, and the wicked will he destroy; and he will spare his people, yea, even if it so be that he must destroy the wicked by fire.

11 And righteousness shall be the girdle of his loins, and faithfulness the girdle of his reins.

Date _____

☐ Completed

12 And then shall the wolf dwell with the lamb; and the leopard shall lie down with the kid, and the calf, and the young lion, and the fatling, together; and a little child shall lead them.

13 And the cow and the bear shall feed; their young ones shall lie down together; and the lion shall eat straw like the ox.

14 And the sucking child shall play on the hole of the asp, and the weaned child shall put his hand on the cockatrice's den.

15 They shall not hurt nor destroy in all my holy mountain; for the earth shall be full of the knowledge of the Lord as the waters cover the sea.

16 Wherefore, the things of all nations shall be made known; yea, all things shall be made known unto the children of men.

17 There is nothing which is secret save it shall be revealed; there is no work of darkness save it shall be made manifest in the light; and there is nothing which is sealed upon the earth save it shall be loosed.

18 Wherefore, all things which have been revealed unto the children of men shall at that day be revealed; and Satan shall have power over the hearts of the children of men no more, for a long time. And now, my beloved brethren, I make an end of my sayings.

Date _____

☐ Completed

2 Nephi 31

1 And now I, Nephi, make an end of my prophesying unto you, my beloved brethren. And I cannot write but a few things, which I know must surely come to pass; neither can I write but a few of the words of my brother Jacob.

2 Wherefore, the things which I have written sufficeth me, save it be a few words which I must speak concerning the doctrine of Christ; wherefore, I shall speak unto you plainly, according to the plainness of my prophesying.

3 For my soul delighteth in plainness; for after this manner doth the Lord God work among the children of men. For the Lord God giveth light unto the understanding; for he speaketh unto men according to their language, unto their understanding.

4 Wherefore, I would that ye should remember that I have spoken unto you concerning that prophet which the Lord showed unto me, that should baptize the Lamb of God, which should take away the sins of the world.

5 And now, if the Lamb of God, he being holy, should have need to be baptized by water, to fulfil all righteousness, O then, how much more need have we, being unholy, to be baptized, yea, even by water!

6 And now, I would ask of you, my beloved brethren, wherein the Lamb of God did fulfil all righteousness in being baptized by water?

Date _____
☐ Completed

7 Know ye not that he was holy? But notwithstanding he being holy, he showeth unto the children of men that, according to the flesh he humbleth himself before the Father, and witnesseth unto the Father that he would be obedient unto him in keeping his commandments.

8 Wherefore, after he was baptized with water the Holy Ghost descended upon him in the form of a dove.

9 And again, it showeth unto the children of men the straitness of the path, and the narrowness of the gate, by which they should enter, he having set the example before them.

10 And he said unto the children of men: Follow thou me. Wherefore, my beloved brethren, can we follow Jesus save we shall be willing to keep the commandments of the Father?

11 And the Father said: Repent ye, repent ye, and be baptized in the name of my Beloved Son.

12 And also, the voice of the Son came unto me, saying: He that is baptized in my name, to him will the Father give the Holy Ghost, like unto me; wherefore, follow me, and do the things which ye have seen me do.

Date _____
☐ Completed

13 Wherefore, my beloved brethren, I know that if ye shall follow the Son, with full purpose of heart, acting no hypocrisy and no deception

before God, but with real intent, repenting of your sins, witnessing unto the Father that ye are willing to take upon you the name of Christ, by baptism—yea, by following your Lord and your Savior down into the water, according to his word, behold, then shall ye receive the Holy Ghost; yea, then cometh the baptism of fire and of the Holy Ghost; and then can ye speak with the tongue of angels, and shout praises unto the Holy One of Israel.

14 But, behold, my beloved brethren, thus came the voice of the Son unto me, saying: After ye have repented of your sins, and witnessed unto the Father that ye are willing to keep my commandments, by the baptism of water, and have received the baptism of fire and of the Holy Ghost, and can speak with a new tongue, yea, even with the tongue of angels, and after this should deny me, it would have been better for you that ye had not known me.

15 And I heard a voice from the Father, saying: Yea, the words of my Beloved are true and faithful. He that endureth to the end, the same shall be saved.

16 And now, my beloved brethren, I know by this that unless a man shall endure to the end, in following the example of the Son of the living God, he cannot be saved.

17 Wherefore, do the things which I have told you I have seen that your Lord and your Redeemer should do; for, for this cause have they been shown unto me, that ye might know the gate by which ye should enter. For the gate by which ye should enter is repentance and baptism by water; and then cometh a remission of your sins by fire and by the Holy Ghost.

18 And then are ye in this strait and narrow path which leads to eternal life; yea, ye have entered in by the gate; ye have done according to the commandments of the Father and the Son; and ye have received the Holy Ghost, which witnesses of the Father and the Son, unto the fulfilling of the promise which he hath made, that if ye entered in by the way ye should receive.

20 Wherefore, ye must press forward with a steadfastness in Christ, having a perfect brightness of hope, and a love of God and of all men. Wherefore, if ye shall press forward, feasting upon the word of Christ, and endure to the end, behold, thus saith the Father: Ye shall have eternal life.

21 And now, behold, my beloved brethren, this is the way; and there is none other way nor name given under heaven whereby man can be saved in the kingdom of God. And now, behold, this is the doctrine of Christ, and the only and true doctrine of the Father, and of the Son, and of the Holy Ghost, which is one God, without end. Amen.

Date _____
☐ Completed

Date _____
☐ Completed

2 Nephi 32

1 And now, behold, my beloved brethren, I suppose that ye ponder somewhat in your hearts concerning that which ye should do after ye have entered in by the way. But, behold, why do ye ponder these things in your hearts?

2 Do ye not remember that I said unto you that after ye had received the Holy Ghost ye could speak with the tongue of angels? And now, how could ye speak with the tongue of angels save it were by the Holy Ghost?

3 Angels speak by the power of the Holy Ghost; wherefore, they speak the words of Christ. Wherefore, I said unto you, feast upon the words of Christ; for behold, the words of Christ will tell you all things what ye should do.

4 Wherefore, now after I have spoken these words, if ye cannot understand them it will be because ye ask not, neither do ye knock; wherefore, ye are not brought into the light, but must perish in the dark.

5 For behold, again I say unto you that if ye will enter in by the way, and receive the Holy Ghost, it will show unto you all things what ye should do.

Date _____
☐ Completed

6 Behold, this is the doctrine of Christ, and there will be no more doctrine given until after he shall manifest himself unto you in the flesh. And when he shall manifest himself unto you in the flesh, the things which he shall say unto you shall ye observe to do.

7 And now I, Nephi, cannot say more; the Spirit stoppeth mine utterance, and I am left to mourn because of the unbelief, and the wickedness, and the ignorance, and the stiffneckedness of men; for they will not search knowledge, nor understand great knowledge, when it is given unto them in plainness, even as plain as word can be.

8 And now, my beloved brethren, I perceive that ye ponder still in your hearts; and it grieveth me that I must speak concerning this thing. For if ye would hearken unto the Spirit which teacheth a man to pray ye would know that ye must pray; for the evil spirit teacheth not a man to pray, but teacheth him that he must not pray.

9 But behold, I say unto you that ye must pray always, and not faint; that ye must not perform any thing unto the Lord save in the first place ye shall pray unto the Father in the name of Christ, that he will consecrate thy performance unto thee, that thy performance may be for the welfare of thy soul.

Date _____
☐ Completed

2 Nephi

Chapter 33—Review

Sight (Memorization) Words

few	death	among	down	know	any

Pattern Word

Pattern word	-ake	-age	-ade	-ame	-ate	-ave
Key words reviewed	take, make	rage	made	came	gate	save

Phonics Application

- *Long Vowel Sounds:* the long sound of vowels make the sound of the letter.
  - The long sound of A (example: **a**te)
  - The long sound of E (example: h**e**re)
- *The Silent E rule:* when an E is at the end of a word, the E is silent and it makes the vowel to the left say its name. (When other rules apply to the word, a word that ends in E is still silent, for example: serve [see R-Controlled Vowels].)
- *Consonant-Vowel-Blend and Blend-Vowel-Blend*: these patterns are the merging together of sounds to make words. A blend is the combination of two (or more) consonants together. These are the blends: BL, CL, FL, GL, PL, SL, BR, CR, DR, FR, GR, PR, TR, SC, SK, SM, SN, SP, ST, SW, TW.
- *Consonant Diagraphs*: diagraphs are two letters that make one sound. The diagraphs are TH, CH, SH, WH.
- *Complex Consonants*: blends that include three consonants, two consonants that sounds like a single letter, and consonant and vowel clusters. The complex consonants are QU, TCH, CK.

Recommended (Age Appropriate) Reading Chunks

- Verses 1–5
- Verses 6–10
- Verses 11–15

Gospel Principle Review/Activity

- How does Nephi feel about what he wrote?
- Why does Nephi cry?
- Who does Nephi have charity for?
- Why is Nephi's voice "crying from the dust"?
- ***Activity:*** What is the judgment bar? Meet with a lawyer or a judge to have them show or explain to you what they do.

Word Patterns—Review

Find the words in the word box in the word search.

M	K	J	E	E	V	V	M	K	L
O	R	V	E	F	J	A	B	J	A
Y	A	T	K	N	A	A	A	W	T
S	I	R	A	I	M	M	F	B	E
J	Y	Z	R	F	K	D	E	P	H
F	P	E	Z	Y	Z	M	R	E	X
B	M	G	U	Y	Q	T	R	T	D
D	D	C	S	Q	B	E	G	P	G
U	T	M	A	D	E	D	T	J	V
V	H	C	U	Z	G	F	B	W	A

Word Box

rake
save
made
fame
late
here

27

2 Nephi 33

1 And now I, Nephi, cannot write all the things which were taught among my people; neither am I mighty in writing, like unto speaking; for when a man speaketh by the power of the Holy Ghost the power of the Holy Ghost carrieth it unto the hearts of the children of men.

2 But behold, there are many that harden their hearts against the Holy Spirit, that it hath no place in them; wherefore, they cast many things away which are written and esteem them as things of naught.

3 But I, Nephi, have written what I have written, and I esteem it as of great worth, and especially unto my people. For I pray continually for them by day, and mine eyes water my pillow by night, because of them; and I cry unto my God in faith, and I know that he will hear my cry.

4 And I know that the Lord God will consecrate my prayers for the gain of my people. And the words which I have written in weakness will be made strong unto them; for it persuadeth them to do good; it maketh known unto them of their fathers; and it speaketh of Jesus, and persuadeth them to believe in him, and to endure to the end, which is life eternal.

5 And it speaketh harshly against sin, according to the plainness of the truth; wherefore, no man will be angry at the words which I have written save he shall be of the spirit of the devil.

6 I glory in plainness; I glory in truth; I glory in my Jesus, for he hath redeemed my soul from hell.

7 I have charity for my people, and great faith in Christ that I shall meet many souls spotless at his judgment-seat.

8 I have charity for the Jew—I say Jew, because I mean them from whence I came.

9 I also have charity for the Gentiles. But behold, for none of these can I hope except they shall be reconciled unto Christ, and enter into the narrow gate, and walk in the strait path which leads to life, and continue in the path until the end of the day of probation.

10 And now, my beloved brethren, and also Jew, and all ye ends of the earth, hearken unto these words and believe in Christ; and if ye believe not in these words believe in Christ. And if ye shall believe in Christ ye will believe in these words, for they are the words of Christ, and he hath given them unto me; and they teach all men that they should do good.

11 And if they are not the words of Christ, judge ye—for Christ will show unto you, with power and great glory, that they are his words, at the last day; and you and I shall stand face to face before his bar; and ye shall know that I have been commanded of him to write these things, notwithstanding my weakness.

Date _____
☐ Completed

Date _____
☐ Completed

12 And I pray the Father in the name of Christ that many of us, if not all, may be saved in his kingdom at that great and last day.

13 And now, my beloved brethren, all those who are of the house of Israel, and all ye ends of the earth, I speak unto you as the voice of one crying from the dust: Farewell until that great day shall come.

14 And you that will not partake of the goodness of God, and respect the words of the Jews, and also my words, and the words which shall proceed forth out of the mouth of the Lamb of God, behold, I bid you an everlasting farewell, for these words shall condemn you at the last day.

15 For what I seal on earth, shall be brought against you at the judgment bar; for thus hath the Lord commanded me, and I must obey. Amen.

Date _____

☐ Completed

Jacob

Chapter 1

Sight (Memorization) Words

most

Word Pattern

Pattern	-ese
Pattern words in scriptures	**these**
Location in chapter	Verses 1–4, 14, 17
Exceptions to the rule	bees, keys, knees, peas, tease, wheeze, please, sleaze, breeze, freeze, sneeze, tweeze
Other words made from this pattern not found in chapter	(none listed)

Phonics Application

- *Long Vowel Sounds:* the long sound of vowels make the sound of the letter.
  - The long sound of E (example: here)
- *The Silent E rule:* when an E is at the end of a word, the E is silent and it makes the vowel to the left say its name. (When other rules apply to the word, a word that ends in E is still silent, for example: serve [see R-controlled vowels].)
- *Consonant-Vowel-Blend and Blend-Vowel-Blend:* these patterns are the merging together of sounds to make words. A blend is the combination of two (or more) consonants together. These are the blends: BL, CL, FL, GL, PL, SL, BR, CR, DR, FR, GR, PR, TR, SC, SK, SM, SN, SP, ST, SW, TW.
- *Consonant Diagraphs:* diagraphs are two letters that make one sound. The diagraphs are TH, CH, SH, WH.
- *Complex Consonants:* blends that include three consonants, two consonants that sounds like a single letter, and consonant and vowel clusters. The complex consonants are QU, TCH, CK.

Recommended (Age Appropriate) Reading Chunks

- Verses 1–5
- Verses 6–10
- Verses 11–19

Gospel Principle Review/Activity

- What did Joseph and Jacob try to teach people?
- What are the two different plates he is talking about? (Refer to the introduction pages of the Book of Mormon.)
- Who is in charge when Nephi dies?
- *Activity:* The people loved Nephi so much that they named all their future kings Nephi in his honor. What are some objects or places that we name after people? How were these people chosen to have such an honor?

Word Patterns

_ese

Words made with –ese word pattern.
Use alphabet letters to create words.

Jacob 1

1 For behold, it came to pass that fifty and five years had passed away from the time that Lehi left Jerusalem; wherefore, Nephi gave me, Jacob, a commandment concerning the small plates, upon which these things are engraven.

2 And he gave me, Jacob, a commandment that I should write upon these plates a few of the things which I considered to be most precious; that I should not touch, save it were lightly, concerning the history of this people which are called the people of Nephi.

3 For he said that the history of his people should be engraven upon his other plates, and that I should preserve these plates and hand them down unto my seed, from generation to generation.

4 And if there were preaching which was sacred, or revelation which was great, or prophesying, that I should engraven the heads of them upon these plates, and touch upon them as much as it were possible, for Christ's sake, and for the sake of our people.

5 For because of faith and great anxiety, it truly had been made manifest unto us concerning our people, what things should happen unto them.

6 And we also had many revelations, and the spirit of much prophecy; wherefore, we knew of Christ and his kingdom, which should come.

7 Wherefore we labored diligently among our people, that we might persuade them to come unto Christ, and partake of the goodness of God, that they might enter into his rest, lest by any means he should swear in his wrath they should not enter in, as in the provocation in the days of temptation while the children of Israel were in the wilderness.

8 Wherefore, we would to God that we could persuade all men not to rebel against God, to provoke him to anger, but that all men would believe in Christ, and view his death, and suffer his cross and bear the shame of the world; wherefore, I, Jacob, take it upon me to fulfil the commandment of my brother Nephi.

9 Now Nephi began to be old, and he saw that he must soon die; wherefore, he anointed a man to be a king and a ruler over his people now, according to the reigns of the kings.

10 The people having loved Nephi exceedingly, he having been a great protector for them, having wielded the sword of Laban in their defence, and having labored in all his days for their welfare—

11 Wherefore, the people were desirous to retain in remembrance his name. And whoso should reign in his stead were called by the people, second Nephi, third Nephi, and so forth, according to the reigns of the kings; and thus they were called by the people, let them be of whatever name they would.

Date _____
☐ Completed

Date _____
☐ Completed

12 And it came to pass that Nephi died.

13 Now the people which were not Lamanites were Nephites; nevertheless, they were called Nephites, Jacobites, Josephites, Zoramites, Lamanites, Lemuelites, and Ishmaelites.

14 But I, Jacob, shall not hereafter distinguish them by these names, but I shall call them Lamanites that seek to destroy the people of Nephi, and those who are friendly to Nephi I shall call Nephites, or the people of Nephi, according to the reigns of the kings.

15 And now it came to pass that the people of Nephi, under the reign of the second king, began to grow hard in their hearts, and indulge themselves somewhat in wicked practices, such as like unto David of old desiring many wives and concubines, and also Solomon, his son.

16 Yea, and they also began to search much gold and silver, and began to be lifted up somewhat in pride.

17 Wherefore I, Jacob, gave unto them these words as I taught them in the temple, having first obtained mine errand from the Lord.

18 For I, Jacob, and my brother Joseph had been consecrated priests and teachers of this people, by the hand of Nephi.

19 And we did magnify our office unto the Lord, taking upon us the responsibility, answering the sins of the people upon our own heads if we did not teach them the word of God with all diligence; wherefore, by laboring with our might their blood might not come upon our garments; otherwise their blood would come upon our garments, and we would not be found spotless at the last day.

Date _____

☐ Completed

Jacob

Chapter 2

Sight (Memorization) Words

some

Word Pattern

Pattern	-ide
Pattern words in scriptures	**pride**
Location in chapter	Verses 13, 16, 20, 22
Other words made from this patterns not found in chapter	hide, ride, side, tide, wide, glide, slide

Phonics Application

- *Long Vowel Sounds:* the long sound of vowels make the sound of the letter.
  - The long sound of I (example: side)
- *The Silent E rule:* when an E is at the end of a word, the E is silent and it makes the vowel to the left say its name. (When other rules apply to the word, a word that ends in E is still silent, for example: serve [see R-controlled vowels].)
- *Consonant-Vowel-Blend and Blend-Vowel-Blend:* these patterns are the merging together of sounds to make words. A blend is the combination of two (or more) consonants together. These are the blends: BL, CL, FL, GL, PL, SL, BR, CR, DR, FR, GR, PR, TR, SC, SK, SM, SN, SP, ST, SW, TW.
- *Consonant Diagraphs:* diagraphs are two letters that make one sound. The diagraphs are TH, CH, SH, WH.
- *Complex Consonants:* blends that include three consonants, two consonants that sounds like a single letter, and consonant and vowel clusters. The complex consonants are QU, TCH, CK.

Recommended (Age Appropriate) Reading Chunks

- Verses 1–6
- Verses 7–10
- Verses 11–15
- Verses 16–22
- Verses 23–29
- Verses 30–35

Gospel Principle Review/Activity

- Why is loving riches dangerous?
- What should men do with their riches?
- *Activity:* If you had one million dollars, what would you do with it? Find ways to spend that money and understand how large this sum is.

Word Patterns

_ide

Words made with –ide word pattern.
Use alphabet letters to create words.

Jacob 2

1 The words which Jacob, the brother of Nephi, spake unto the people of Nephi, after the death of Nephi:

2 Now, my beloved brethren, I, Jacob, according to the responsibility which I am under to God, to magnify mine office with soberness, and that I might rid my garments of your sins, I come up into the temple this day that I might declare unto you the word of God.

3 And ye yourselves know that I have hitherto been diligent in the office of my calling; but I this day am weighed down with much more desire and anxiety for the welfare of your souls than I have hitherto been.

4 For behold, as yet, ye have been obedient unto the word of the Lord, which I have given unto you.

5 But behold, hearken ye unto me, and know that by the help of the all–powerful Creator of heaven and earth I can tell you concerning your thoughts, how that ye are beginning to labor in sin, which sin appeareth very abominable unto me, yea, and abominable unto God.

6 Yea, it grieveth my soul and causeth me to shrink with shame before the presence of my Maker, that I must testify unto you concerning the wickedness of your hearts.

Date _____

☐ Completed

7 And also it grieveth me that I must use so much boldness of speech concerning you, before your wives and your children, many of whose feelings are exceedingly tender and chaste and delicate before God, which thing is pleasing unto God;

8 And it supposeth me that they have come up hither to hear the pleasing word of God, yea, the word which healeth the wounded soul.

9 Wherefore, it burdeneth my soul that I should be constrained, because of the strict commandment which I have received from God, to admonish you according to your crimes, to enlarge the wounds of those who are already wounded, instead of consoling and healing their wounds; and those who have not been wounded, instead of feasting upon the pleasing word of God have daggers placed to pierce their souls and wound their delicate minds.

10 But, notwithstanding the greatness of the task, I must do according to the strict commands of God, and tell you concerning your wickedness and abominations, in the presence of the pure in heart, and the broken heart, and under the glance of the piercing eye of the Almighty God.

Date _____

☐ Completed

11 Wherefore, I must tell you the truth according to the plainness of the word of God. For behold, as I inquired of the Lord, thus came the word unto me, saying: Jacob, get thou up into the temple on the morrow, and declare the word which I shall give thee unto this people.

12 And now behold, my brethren, this is the word which I declare unto you, that many of you have begun to search for gold, and for silver, and for all manner of precious ores, in the which this land, which is a land of promise unto you and to your seed, doth abound most plentifully.

13 And the hand of providence hath smiled upon you most pleasingly, that you have obtained many riches; and because some of you have obtained more abundantly than that of your brethren ye are lifted up in the pride of your hearts, and wear stiff necks and high heads because of the costliness of your apparel, and persecute your brethren because ye suppose that ye are better than they.

14 And now, my brethren, do ye suppose that God justifieth you in this thing? Behold, I say unto you, Nay. But he condemneth you, and if ye persist in these things his judgments must speedily come unto you.

15 O that he would show you that he can pierce you, and with one glance of his eye he can smite you to the dust!

16 O that he would rid you from this iniquity and abomination. And, O that ye would listen unto the word of his commands, and let not this pride of your hearts destroy your souls!

17 Think of your brethren like unto yourselves, and be familiar with all and free with your substance, that they may be rich like unto you.

18 But before ye seek for riches, seek ye for the kingdom of God.

19 And after ye have obtained a hope in Christ ye shall obtain riches, if ye seek them; and ye will seek them for the intent to do good—to clothe the naked, and to feed the hungry, and to liberate the captive, and administer relief to the sick and the afflicted.

20 And now, my brethren, I have spoken unto you concerning pride; and those of you which have afflicted your neighbor, and persecuted him because ye were proud in your hearts, of the things which God hath given you, what say ye of it?

21 Do ye not suppose that such things are abominable unto him who created all flesh? And the one being is as precious in his sight as the other. And all flesh is of the dust; and for the selfsame end hath he created them, that they should keep his commandments and glorify him forever.

22 And now I make an end of speaking unto you concerning this pride. And were it not that I must speak unto you concerning a grosser crime, my heart would rejoice exceedingly because of you.

23 But the word of God burdens me because of your grosser crimes. For behold, thus saith the Lord: This people begin to wax in iniquity; they understand not the scriptures, for they seek to excuse themselves in committing whoredoms, because of the things which were written concerning David, and Solomon his son.

24 Behold, David and Solomon truly had many wives and concubines,

Notes

Date _____

☐ Completed

Date _____

☐ Completed

37

which thing was abominable before me, saith the Lord.

25 Wherefore, thus saith the Lord, I have led this people forth out of the land of Jerusalem, by the power of mine arm, that I might raise up unto me a righteous branch from the fruit of the loins of Joseph.

26 Wherefore, I the Lord God will not suffer that this people shall do like unto them of old.

27 Wherefore, my brethren, hear me, and hearken to the word of the Lord: For there shall not any man among you have save it be one wife; and concubines he shall have none;

28 For I, the Lord God, delight in the chastity of women. And whoredoms are an abomination before me; thus saith the Lord of Hosts.

29 Wherefore, this people shall keep my commandments, saith the Lord of Hosts, or cursed be the land for their sakes.

30 For if I will, saith the Lord of Hosts, raise up seed unto me, I will command my people; otherwise they shall hearken unto these things.

31 For behold, I, the Lord, have seen the sorrow, and heard the mourning of the daughters of my people in the land of Jerusalem, yea, and in all the lands of my people, because of the wickedness and abominations of their husbands.

32 And I will not suffer, saith the Lord of Hosts, that the cries of the fair daughters of this people, which I have led out of the land of Jerusalem, shall come up unto me against the men of my people, saith the Lord of Hosts.

33 For they shall not lead away captive the daughters of my people because of their tenderness, save I shall visit them with a sore curse, even unto destruction; for they shall not commit whoredoms, like unto them of old, saith the Lord of Hosts.

34 And now behold, my brethren, ye know that these commandments were given to our father, Lehi; wherefore, ye have known them before; and ye have come unto great condemnation; for ye have done these things which ye ought not to have done.

35 Behold, ye have done greater iniquities than the Lamanites, our brethren. Ye have broken the hearts of your tender wives, and lost the confidence of your children, because of your bad examples before them; and the sobbings of their hearts ascend up to God against you. And because of the strictness of the word of God, which cometh down against you, many hearts died, pierced with deep wounds.

Date _____
☐ Completed

Date _____
☐ Completed

Jacob

Chapter 3

Sight (Memorization) Words

how

Word Pattern

Pattern	-ike
Pattern words in scriptures	like
Location in chapter	Verse 3
Exceptions to the rule	Nike
Other words made from this patterns not found in chapter	bike, hike, Mike, pike, spike

Phonics Application

- *Long Vowel Sounds:* the long sound of vowels make the sound of the letter.
  - The long sound of I (example: s**i**de)
- *The Silent E rule:* when an E is at the end of a word, the E is silent and it makes the vowel to the left say its name. (When other rules apply to the word, a word that ends in E is still silent, for example: serve [see R-controlled vowels].)
- *Consonant-Vowel-Blend and Blend-Vowel-Blend:* these patterns are the merging together of sounds to make words. A blend is the combination of two (or more) consonants together. These are the blends: BL, CL, FL, GL, PL, SL, BR, CR, DR, FR, GR, PR, TR, SC, SK, SM, SN, SP, ST, SW, TW.
- *Consonant Diagraphs:* diagraphs are two letters that make one sound. The diagraphs are TH, CH, SH, WH.
- *Complex Consonants:* blends that include three consonants, two consonants that sounds like a single letter, and consonant and vowel clusters. The complex consonants are QU, TCH, CK.

Recommended (Age Appropriate) Reading Chunks

- Verses 1–5
- Verses 6–9
- Verses 10–14

Gospel Principle Review/Activity

- What does it mean to be "pure in heart"? What do the "pure in heart" receive?
- *Activity:* In this chapter, Jacob is warning his people against evil things.
  - Can you find warning signs in your community?
  - Can you find warning signs at home?
  - Can you find warning signs at church?
  - What are these signs warning you of?

Word Patterns

___ike

Words made with –ike word pattern.
Use alphabet letters to create words.

Jacob 3

1 But behold, I, Jacob, would speak unto you that are pure in heart. Look unto God with firmness of mind, and pray unto him with exceeding faith, and he will console you in your afflictions, and he will plead your cause, and send down justice upon those who seek your destruction.

2 O all ye that are pure in heart, lift up your heads and receive the pleasing word of God, and feast upon his love; for ye may, if your minds are firm, forever.

3 But, wo, wo, unto you that are not pure in heart, that are filthy this day before God; for except ye repent the land is cursed for your sakes; and the Lamanites, which are not filthy like unto you, nevertheless they are cursed with a sore cursing, shall scourge you even unto destruction.

4 And the time speedily cometh, that except ye repent they shall possess the land of your inheritance, and the Lord God will lead away the righteous out from among you.

5 Behold, the Lamanites your brethren, whom ye hate because of their filthiness and the cursing which hath come upon their skins, are more righteous than you; for they have not forgotten the commandment of the Lord, which was given unto our father—that they should have save it were one wife, and concubines they should have none, and there should not be whoredoms committed among them.

6 And now, this commandment they observe to keep; wherefore, because of this observance, in keeping this commandment, the Lord God will not destroy them, but will be merciful unto them; and one day they shall become a blessed people.

7 Behold, their husbands love their wives, and their wives love their husbands; and their husbands and their wives love their children; and their unbelief and their hatred towards you is because of the iniquity of their fathers; wherefore, how much better are you than they, in the sight of your great Creator?

8 O my brethren, I fear that unless ye shall repent of your sins that their skins will be whiter than yours, when ye shall be brought with them before the throne of God.

9 Wherefore, a commandment I give unto you, which is the word of God, that ye revile no more against them because of the darkness of their skins; neither shall ye revile against them because of their filthiness; but ye shall remember your own filthiness, and remember that their filthiness came because of their fathers.

10 Wherefore, ye shall remember your children, how that ye have grieved

Notes

Date _____
☐ Completed

Date _____
☐ Completed

their hearts because of the example that ye have set before them; and also, remember that ye may, because of your filthiness, bring your children unto destruction, and their sins be heaped upon your heads at the last day.

11 O my brethren, hearken unto my words; arouse the faculties of your souls; shake yourselves that ye may awake from the slumber of death; and loose yourselves from the pains of hell that ye may not become angels to the devil, to be cast into that lake of fire and brimstone which is the second death.

12 And now I, Jacob, spake many more things unto the people of Nephi, warning them against fornication and lasciviousness, and every kind of sin, telling them the awful consequences of them.

13 And a hundredth part of the proceedings of this people, which now began to be numerous, cannot be written upon these plates; but many of their proceedings are written upon the larger plates, and their wars, and their contentions, and the reigns of their kings.

14 These plates are called the plates of Jacob, and they were made by the hand of Nephi. And I make an end of speaking these words.

Date _____

☐ Completed

Jacob 4

1 Now behold, it came to pass that I, Jacob, having ministered much unto my people in word, (and I cannot write but a little of my words, because of the difficulty of engraving our words upon plates) and we know that the things which we write upon plates must remain;

2 But whatsoever things we write upon anything save it be upon plates must perish and vanish away; but we can write a few words upon plates, which will give our children, and also our beloved brethren, a small degree of knowledge concerning us, or concerning their fathers—

3 Now in this thing we do rejoice; and we labor diligently to engraven these words upon plates, hoping that our beloved brethren and our children will receive them with thankful hearts, and look upon them that they may learn with joy and not with sorrow, neither with contempt, concerning their first parents.

4 For, for this intent have we written these things, that they may know that we knew of Christ, and we had a hope of his glory many hundred years before his coming; and not only we ourselves had a hope of his glory, but also all the holy prophets which were before us.

5 Behold, they believed in Christ and worshiped the Father in his name, and also we worship the Father in his name. And for this intent we keep the law of Moses, it pointing our souls to him; and for this cause it is sanctified unto us for righteousness, even as it was accounted unto Abraham in the wilderness to be obedient unto the commands of God in offering up his son Isaac, which is a similitude of God and his Only Begotten Son.

6 Wherefore, we search the prophets, and we have many revelations and the spirit of prophecy; and having all these witnesses we obtain a hope, and our faith becometh unshaken, insomuch that we truly can command in the name of Jesus and the very trees obey us, or the mountains, or the waves of the sea.

7 Nevertheless, the Lord God showeth us our weakness that we may know that it is by his grace, and his great condescensions unto the children of men, that we have power to do these things.

8 Behold, great and marvelous are the works of the Lord. How unsearchable are the depths of the mysteries of him; and it is impossible that man should find out all his ways. And no man knoweth of his ways save it be revealed unto him; wherefore, brethren, despise not the revelations of God.

9 For behold, by the power of his word man came upon the face of the earth, which earth was created by the power of his word. Wherefore, if

Date _____
☐ Completed

Date _____
☐ Completed

God being able to speak and the world was, and to speak and man was created, O then, why not able to command the earth, or the workmanship of his hands upon the face of it, according to his will and pleasure?

10 Wherefore, brethren, seek not to counsel the Lord, but to take counsel from his hand. For behold, ye yourselves know that he counseleth in wisdom, and in justice, and in great mercy, over all his works.

11 Wherefore, beloved brethren, be reconciled unto him through the atonement of Christ, his Only Begotten Son, and ye may obtain a resurrection, according to the power of the resurrection which is in Christ, and be presented as the first-fruits of Christ unto God, having faith, and obtained a good hope of glory in him before he manifesteth himself in the flesh.

12 And now, beloved, marvel not that I tell you these things; for why not speak of the atonement of Christ, and attain to a perfect knowledge of him, as to attain to the knowledge of a resurrection and the world to come?

13 Behold, my brethren, he that prophesieth, let him prophesy to the understanding of men; for the Spirit speaketh the truth and lieth not. Wherefore, it speaketh of things as they really are, and of things as they really will be; wherefore, these things are manifested unto us plainly, for the salvation of our souls. But behold, we are not witnesses alone in these things; for God also spake them unto prophets of old.

14 But behold, the Jews were a stiffnecked people; and they despised the words of plainness, and killed the prophets, and sought for things that they could not understand. Wherefore, because of their blindness, which blindness came by looking beyond the mark, they must needs fall; for God hath taken away his plainness from them, and delivered unto them many things which they cannot understand, because they desired it. And because they desired it God hath done it, that they may stumble.

15 And now I, Jacob, am led on by the Spirit unto prophesying; for I perceive by the workings of the Spirit which is in me, that by the stumbling of the Jews they will reject the stone upon which they might build and have safe foundation.

16 But behold, according to the scriptures, this stone shall become the great, and the last, and the only sure foundation, upon which the Jews can build.

17 And now, my beloved, how is it possible that these, after having rejected the sure foundation, can ever build upon it, that it may become the head of their corner?

18 Behold, my beloved brethren, I will unfold this mystery unto you; if I do not, by any means, get shaken from my firmness in the Spirit, and stumble because of my over anxiety for you.

Notes

46

Jacob 5

1 Behold, my brethren, do ye not remember to have read the words of the prophet Zenos, which he spake unto the house of Israel, saying:

2 Hearken, O ye house of Israel, and hear the words of me, a prophet of the Lord.

3 For behold, thus saith the Lord, I will liken thee, O house of Israel, like unto a tame olive-tree, which a man took and nourished in his vineyard; and it grew, and waxed old, and began to decay.

4 And it came to pass that the master of the vineyard went forth, and he saw that his olive-tree began to decay; and he said: I will prune it, and dig about it, and nourish it, that perhaps it may shoot forth young and tender branches, and it perish not.

5 And it came to pass that he pruned it, and digged about it, and nourished it according to his word.

6 And it came to pass that after many days it began to put forth somewhat a little, young and tender branches; but behold, the main top thereof began to perish.

Date _____
☐ Completed

7 And it came to pass that the master of the vineyard saw it, and he said unto his servant: It grieveth me that I should lose this tree; wherefore, go and pluck the branches from a wild olive-tree, and bring them hither unto me; and we will pluck off those main branches which are beginning to wither away, and we will cast them into the fire that they may be burned.

8 And behold, saith the Lord of the vineyard, I take away many of these young and tender branches, and I will graft them whithersoever I will; and it mattereth not that if it so be that the root of this tree will perish, I may preserve the fruit thereof unto myself; wherefore, I will take these young and tender branches, and I will graft them whithersoever I will.

9 Take thou the branches of the wild olive-tree, and graft them in, in the stead thereof; and these which I have plucked off I will cast into the fire and burn them, that they may not cumber the ground of my vineyard.

10 And it came to pass that the servant of the Lord of the vineyard did according to the word of the Lord of the vineyard, and grafted in the branches of the wild olive-tree.

11 And the Lord of the vineyard caused that it should be digged about, and pruned, and nourished, saying unto his servant: It grieveth me that I should lose this tree; wherefore, that perhaps I might preserve the roots thereof that they perish not, that I might preserve them unto myself, I have done this thing.

Date _____
☐ Completed

12 Wherefore, go thy way; watch the tree, and nourish it, according to my words.

13 And these will I place in the nethermost part of my vineyard, whithersoever I will, it mattereth not unto thee; and I do it that I may preserve unto myself the natural branches of the tree; and also, that I may lay up fruit thereof against the season, unto myself; for it grieveth me that I should lose this tree and the fruit thereof.

14 And it came to pass that the Lord of the vineyard went his way, and hid the natural branches of the tame olive-tree in the nethermost parts of the vineyard, some in one and some in another, according to his will and pleasure.

15 And it came to pass that a long time passed away, and the Lord of the vineyard said unto his servant: Come, let us go down into the vineyard, that we may labor in the vineyard.

16 And it came to pass that the Lord of the vineyard, and also the servant, went down into the vineyard to labor. And it came to pass that the servant said unto his master: Behold, look here; behold the tree.

17 And it came to pass that the Lord of the vineyard looked and beheld the tree in the which the wild olive branches had been grafted; and it had sprung forth and begun to bear fruit. And he beheld that it was good; and the fruit thereof was like unto the natural fruit.

18 And he said unto the servant: Behold, the branches of the wild tree have taken hold of the moisture of the root thereof, that the root thereof hath brought forth much strength; and because of the much strength of the root thereof the wild branches have brought forth tame fruit. Now, if we had not grafted in these branches, the tree thereof would have perished. And now, behold, I shall lay up much fruit, which the tree thereof hath brought forth; and the fruit thereof I shall lay up against the season, unto mine own self.

19 And it came to pass that the Lord of the vineyard said unto the servant: Come, let us go to the nethermost part of the vineyard, and behold if the natural branches of the tree have not brought forth much fruit also, that I may lay up of the fruit thereof against the season, unto mine own self.

20 And it came to pass that they went forth whither the master had hid the natural branches of the tree, and he said unto the servant: Behold these; and he beheld the first that it had brought forth much fruit; and he beheld also that it was good. And he said unto the servant: Take of the fruit thereof, and lay it up against the season, that I may preserve it unto mine own self; for behold, said he, this long time have I nourished it, and it hath brought forth much fruit.

21 And it came to pass that the servant said unto his master: How comest thou hither to plant this tree, or this branch of the tree? For behold, it was the poorest spot in all the land of thy vineyard.

Notes

Date _____
☐ Completed

Date _____
☐ Completed

22 And the Lord of the vineyard said unto him: Counsel me not; I knew that it was a poor spot of ground; wherefore, I said unto thee, I have nourished it this long time, and thou beholdest that it hath brought forth much fruit.

23 And it came to pass that the Lord of the vineyard said unto his servant: Look hither; behold I have planted another branch of the tree also; and thou knowest that this spot of ground was poorer than the first. But, behold the tree. I have nourished it this long time, and it hath brought forth much fruit; therefore, gather it, and lay it up against the season, that I may preserve it unto mine own self.

24 And it came to pass that the Lord of the vineyard said again unto his servant: Look hither, and behold another branch also, which I have planted; behold that I have nourished it also, and it hath brought forth fruit.

25 And he said unto the servant: Look hither and behold the last. Behold, this have I planted in a good spot of ground; and I have nourished it this long time, and only a part of the tree hath brought forth tame fruit, and the other part of the tree hath brought forth wild fruit; behold, I have nourished this tree like unto the others.

26 And it came to pass that the Lord of the vineyard said unto the servant: Pluck off the branches that have not brought forth good fruit, and cast them into the fire.

27 But behold, the servant said unto him: Let us prune it, and dig about it, and nourish it a little longer, that perhaps it may bring forth good fruit unto thee, that thou canst lay it up against the season.

28 And it came to pass that the Lord of the vineyard and the servant of the Lord of the vineyard did nourish all the fruit of the vineyard.

29 And it came to pass that a long time had passed away, and the Lord of the vineyard said unto his servant: Come, let us go down into the vineyard, that we may labor again in the vineyard. For behold, the time draweth near, and the end soon cometh; wherefore, I must lay up fruit against the season, unto mine own self.

30 And it came to pass that the Lord of the vineyard and the servant went down into the vineyard; and they came to the tree whose natural branches had been broken off, and the wild branches had been grafted in; and behold all sorts of fruit did cumber the tree.

31 And it came to pass that the Lord of the vineyard did taste of the fruit, every sort according to its number. And the Lord of the vineyard said: Behold, this long time have we nourished this tree, and I have laid up unto myself against the season much fruit.

32 But behold, this time it hath brought forth much fruit, and there is none of it which is good. And behold, there are all kinds of bad fruit;

Date _____
☐ Completed

Date _____
☐ Completed

and it profiteth me nothing, notwithstanding all our labor; and now it grieveth me that I should lose this tree.

33 And the Lord of the vineyard said unto the servant: What shall we do unto the tree, that I may preserve again good fruit thereof unto mine own self?

34 And the servant said unto his master: Behold, because thou didst graft in the branches of the wild olive-tree they have nourished the roots, that they are alive and they have not perished; wherefore thou beholdest that they are yet good.

35 And it came to pass that the Lord of the vineyard said unto his servant: The tree profiteth me nothing, and the roots thereof profit me nothing so long as it shall bring forth evil fruit.

36 Nevertheless, I know that the roots are good, and for mine own purpose I have preserved them; and because of their much strength they have hitherto brought forth, from the wild branches, good fruit.

37 But behold, the wild branches have grown and have overrun the roots thereof; and because that the wild branches have overcome the roots thereof it hath brought forth much evil fruit; and because that it hath brought forth so much evil fruit thou beholdest that it beginneth to perish; and it will soon become ripened, that it may be cast into the fire, except we should do something for it to preserve it.

38 And it came to pass that the Lord of the vineyard said unto his servant: Let us go down into the nethermost parts of the vineyard, and behold if the natural branches have also brought forth evil fruit.

39 And it came to pass that they went down into the nethermost parts of the vineyard. And it came to pass that they beheld that the fruit of the natural branches had become corrupt also; yea, the first and the second and also the last; and they had all become corrupt.

40 And the wild fruit of the last had overcome that part of the tree which brought forth good fruit, even that the branch had withered away and died.

41 And it came to pass that the Lord of the vineyard wept, and said unto the servant: What could I have done more for my vineyard?

42 Behold, I knew that all the fruit of the vineyard, save it were these, had become corrupted. And now these which have once brought forth good fruit have also become corrupted; and now all the trees of my vineyard are good for nothing save it be to be hewn down and cast into the fire.

43 And behold this last, whose branch hath withered away, I did plant in a good spot of ground; yea, even that which was choice unto me above all other parts of the land of my vineyard.

44 And thou beheldest that I also cut down that which cumbered this spot of ground, that I might plant this tree in the stead thereof.

Date _____
☐ Completed

Date _____
☐ Completed

45 And thou beheldest that a part thereof brought forth good fruit, and a part thereof brought forth wild fruit; and because I plucked not the branches thereof and cast them into the fire, behold, they have overcome the good branch that it hath withered away.

46 And now, behold, notwithstanding all the care which we have taken of my vineyard, the trees thereof have become corrupted, that they bring forth no good fruit; and these I had hoped to preserve, to have laid up fruit thereof against the season, unto mine own self. But, behold, they have become like unto the wild olive-tree, and they are of no worth but to be hewn down and cast into the fire; and it grieveth me that I should lose them.

47 But what could I have done more in my vineyard? Have I slackened mine hand, that I have not nourished it? Nay, I have nourished it, and I have digged about it, and I have pruned it, and I have dunged it; and I have stretched forth mine hand almost all the day long, and the end draweth nigh. And it grieveth me that I should hew down all the trees of my vineyard, and cast them into the fire that they should be burned. Who is it that has corrupted my vineyard?

48 And it came to pass that the servant said unto his master: Is it not the loftiness of thy vineyard—have not the branches thereof overcome the roots which are good? And because the branches have overcome the roots thereof, behold they grew faster than the strength of the roots, taking strength unto themselves. Behold, I say, is not this the cause that the trees of thy vineyard have become corrupted?

49 And it came to pass that the Lord of the vineyard said unto the servant: Let us go to and hew down the trees of the vineyard and cast them into the fire, that they shall not cumber the ground of my vineyard, for I have done all. What could I have done more for my vineyard?

50 But, behold, the servant said unto the Lord of the vineyard: Spare it a little longer.

51 And the Lord said: Yea, I will spare it a little longer, for it grieveth me that I should lose the trees of my vineyard.

52 Wherefore, let us take of the branches of these which I have planted in the nethermost parts of my vineyard, and let us graft them into the tree from whence they came; and let us pluck from the tree those branches whose fruit is most bitter, and graft in the natural branches of the tree in the stead thereof.

53 And this will I do that the tree may not perish, that, perhaps, I may preserve unto myself the roots thereof for mine own purpose.

54 And, behold, the roots of the natural branches of the tree which I planted whithersoever I would are yet alive; wherefore, that I may preserve them also for mine own purpose, I will take of the branches of this

Date _____
☐ Completed

Date _____
☐ Completed

tree, and I will graft them in unto them. Yea, I will graft in unto them the branches of their mother tree, that I may preserve the roots also unto mine own self, that when they shall be sufficiently strong perhaps they may bring forth good fruit unto me, and I may yet have glory in the fruit of my vineyard.

55 And it came to pass that they took from the natural tree which had become wild, and grafted in unto the natural trees, which also had become wild.

56 And they also took of the natural trees which had become wild, and grafted into their mother tree.

57 And the Lord of the vineyard said unto the servant: Pluck not the wild branches from the trees, save it be those which are most bitter; and in them ye shall graft according to that which I have said.

58 And we will nourish again the trees of the vineyard, and we will trim up the branches thereof; and we will pluck from the trees those branches which are ripened, that must perish, and cast them into the fire.

59 And this I do that, perhaps, the roots thereof may take strength because of their goodness; and because of the change of the branches, that the good may overcome the evil.

60 And because that I have preserved the natural branches and the roots thereof, and that I have grafted in the natural branches again into their mother tree, and have preserved the roots of their mother tree, that, perhaps, the trees of my vineyard may bring forth again good fruit and that I may have joy again in the fruit of my vineyard, and, perhaps, that I may rejoice exceedingly that I have preserved the roots and the branches of the first fruit—

61 Wherefore, go to, and call servants, that we may labor diligently with our might in the vineyard, that we may prepare the way, that I may bring forth again the natural fruit, which natural fruit is good and the most precious above all other fruit.

62 Wherefore, let us go to and labor with our might this last time, for behold the end draweth nigh, and this is for the last time that I shall prune my vineyard.

63 Graft in the branches; begin at the last that they may be first, and that the first may be last, and dig about the trees, both old and young, the first and the last; and the last and the first, that all may be nourished once again for the last time.

64 Wherefore, dig about them, and prune them, and dung them once more, for the last time, for the end draweth nigh. And if it be so that these last grafts shall grow, and bring forth the natural fruit, then shall ye prepare the way for them, that they may grow.

65 And as they begin to grow ye shall clear away the branches which bring forth bitter fruit, according to the strength of the good and the size

Date _____
☐ Completed

Date _____
☐ Completed

thereof; and ye shall not clear away the bad thereof all at once, lest the roots thereof should be too strong for the graft, and the graft thereof shall perish, and I lose the trees of my vineyard.

66 For it grieveth me that I should lose the trees of my vineyard; wherefore ye shall clear away the bad according as the good shall grow, that the root and the top may be equal in strength, until the good shall overcome the bad, and the bad be hewn down and cast into the fire, that they cumber not the ground of my vineyard; and thus will I sweep away the bad out of my vineyard.

67 And the branches of the natural tree will I graft in again into the natural tree;

68 And the branches of the natural tree will I graft into the natural branches of the tree; and thus will I bring them together again, that they shall bring forth the natural fruit, and they shall be one.

69 And the bad shall be cast away, yea, even out of all the land of my vineyard; for behold, only this once will I prune my vineyard.

70 And it came to pass that the Lord of the vineyard sent his servant; and the servant went and did as the Lord had commanded him, and brought other servants; and they were few.

71 And the Lord of the vineyard said unto them: Go to, and labor in the vineyard, with your might. For behold, this is the last time that I shall nourish my vineyard; for the end is nigh at hand, and the season speedily cometh; and if ye labor with your might with me ye shall have joy in the fruit which I shall lay up unto myself against the time which will soon come.

72 And it came to pass that the servants did go and labor with their mights; and the Lord of the vineyard labored also with them; and they did obey the commandments of the Lord of the vineyard in all things.

73 And there began to be the natural fruit again in the vineyard; and the natural branches began to grow and thrive exceedingly; and the wild branches began to be plucked off and to be cast away; and they did keep the root and the top thereof equal, according to the strength thereof.

74 And thus they labored, with all diligence, according to the commandments of the Lord of the vineyard, even until the bad had been cast away out of the vineyard, and the Lord had preserved unto himself that the trees had become again the natural fruit; and they became like unto one body; and the fruits were equal; and the Lord of the vineyard had preserved unto himself the natural fruit, which was most precious unto him from the beginning.

75 And it came to pass that when the Lord of the vineyard saw that his fruit was good, and that his vineyard was no more corrupt, he called up his servants, and said unto them: Behold, for this last time have we

Date _____
☐ Completed

Date _____
☐ Completed

nourished my vineyard; and thou beholdest that I have done according to my will; and I have preserved the natural fruit, that it is good, even like as it was in the beginning. And blessed art thou; for because ye have been diligent in laboring with me in my vineyard, and have kept my commandments, and have brought unto me again the natural fruit, that my vineyard is no more corrupted, and the bad is cast away, behold ye shall have joy with me because of the fruit of my vineyard.

76 For behold, for a long time will I lay up of the fruit of my vineyard unto mine own self against the season, which speedily cometh; and for the last time have I nourished my vineyard, and pruned it, and dug about it, and dunged it; wherefore I will lay up unto mine own self of the fruit, for a long time, according to that which I have spoken.

77 And when the time cometh that evil fruit shall again come into my vineyard, then will I cause the good and the bad to be gathered; and the good will I preserve unto myself, and the bad will I cast away into its own place. And then cometh the season and the end; and my vineyard will I cause to be burned with fire.

Date _____

☐ Completed

56

Jacob 6

1 And now, behold, my brethren, as I said unto you that I would prophesy, behold, this is my prophecy—that the things which this prophet Zenos spake, concerning the house of Israel, in the which he likened them unto a tame olive-tree, must surely come to pass.

2 And the day that he shall set his hand again the second time to recover his people, is the day, yea, even the last time, that the servants of the Lord shall go forth in his power, to nourish and prune his vineyard; and after that the end soon cometh.

3 And how blessed are they who have labored diligently in his vineyard; and how cursed are they who shall be cast out into their own place! And the world shall be burned with fire.

4 And how merciful is our God unto us, for he remembereth the house of Israel, both roots and branches; and he stretches forth his hands unto them all the day long; and they are a stiffnecked and a gainsaying people; but as many as will not harden their hearts shall be saved in the kingdom of God.

5 Wherefore, my beloved brethren, I beseech of you in words of soberness that ye would repent, and come with full purpose of heart, and cleave unto God as he cleaveth unto you. And while his arm of mercy is extended towards you in the light of the day, harden not your hearts.

6 Yea, today, if ye will hear his voice, harden not your hearts; for why will ye die?

Date _____
☐ Completed

7 For behold, after ye have been nourished by the good word of God all the day long, will ye bring forth evil fruit, that ye must be hewn down and cast into the fire?

8 Behold, will ye reject these words? Will ye reject the words of the prophets; and will ye reject all the words which have been spoken concerning Christ, after so many have spoken concerning him; and deny the good word of Christ, and the power of God, and the gift of the Holy Ghost, and quench the Holy Spirit, and make a mock of the great plan of redemption, which hath been laid for you?

9 Know ye not that if ye will do these things, that the power of the redemption and the resurrection, which is in Christ, will bring you to stand with shame and awful guilt before the bar of God?

10 And according to the power of justice, for justice cannot be denied, ye must go away into that lake of fire and brimstone, whose flames are unquenchable, and whose smoke ascendeth up forever and ever, which lake of fire and brimstone is endless torment.

11 O then, my beloved brethren, repent ye, and enter in at the strait gate, and continue in the way which is narrow, until ye shall obtain eternal life.

12 O be wise; what can I say more?

13 Finally, I bid you farewell, until I shall meet you before the pleasing bar of God, which bar striketh the wicked with awful dread and fear.

Date _____
☐ Completed

Jacob

Chapter 7

Sight (Memorization) Words

sign

(Note: the -gn rule is explained in Mosiah 16.)

Word Pattern

Pattern	-use
Pattern words in scriptures	**use**
Location in chapter	Verse 4
Exceptions to the rule	lose, blues, bruise, cruise, snooze, choose, shoes
Other words made from this patterns not found in chapter	fuse, muse

Phonics Application

- *Long Vowel Sounds:* the long sound of vowels make the sound of the letter.
  - The long sound of U (example: **u**se)
- *The Silent E rule:* when an E is at the end of a word, the E is silent and it makes the vowel to the left say its name. (When other rules apply to the word, a word that ends in E is still silent, for example: serve [see R-controlled vowels].)
- *Consonant-Vowel-Blend and Blend-Vowel-Blend:* these patterns are the merging together of sounds to make words. A blend is the combination of two (or more) consonants together. These are the blends: BL, CL, FL, GL, PL, SL, BR, CR, DR, FR, GR, PR, TR, SC, SK, SM, SN, SP, ST, SW, TW.
- *Consonant Diagraphs:* diagraphs are two letters that make one sound. The diagraphs are TH, CH, SH, WH.
- *Complex Consonants:* blends that include three consonants, two consonants that sounds like a single letter, and consonant and vowel clusters. The complex consonants are QU, TCH, CK.

Recommended (Age Appropriate) Reading Chunks

- Verses 1–5
- Verses 6–11
- Verses 12–17
- Verses 18–23
- Verses 24–27

Gospel Principle Review/Activity

- What happens when Sherem demands to see a sign from God?
- Who do all the prophets speak of?
- *Activity:* Jacob was great at standing up for truth against someone who didn't believe. Write in your journal some of the things you learned from Jacob about missionary work.

Word Patterns

__use

Words made with –use word pattern.
Use alphabet letters to create words.

Jacob 7

1 And now it came to pass after some years had passed away, there came a man among the people of Nephi, whose name was Sherem.

2 And it came to pass that he began to preach among the people, and to declare unto them that there should be no Christ. And he preached many things which were flattering unto the people; and this he did that he might overthrow the doctrine of Christ.

3 And he labored diligently that he might lead away the hearts of the people, insomuch that he did lead away many hearts; and he knowing that I, Jacob, had faith in Christ who should come, he sought much opportunity that he might come unto me.

4 And he was learned, that he had a perfect knowledge of the language of the people; wherefore, he could use much flattery, and much power of speech, according to the power of the devil.

5 And he had hope to shake me from the faith, notwithstanding the many revelations and the many things which I had seen concerning these things; for I truly had seen angels, and they had ministered unto me. And also, I had heard the voice of the Lord speaking unto me in very word, from time to time; wherefore, I could not be shaken.

Date _____
☐ Completed

6 And it came to pass that he came unto me, and on this wise did he speak unto me, saying: Brother Jacob, I have sought much opportunity that I might speak unto you; for I have heard and also know that thou goest about much, preaching that which ye call the gospel, or the doctrine of Christ.

7 And ye have led away much of this people that they pervert the right way of God, and keep not the law of Moses which is the right way; and convert the law of Moses into the worship of a being which ye say shall come many hundred years hence. And now behold, I, Sherem, declare unto you that this is blasphemy; for no man knoweth of such things; for he cannot tell of things to come. And after this manner did Sherem contend against me.

8 But behold, the Lord God poured in his Spirit into my soul, insomuch that I did confound him in all his words.

9 And I said unto him: Deniest thou the Christ who shall come? And he said: If there should be a Christ, I would not deny him; but I know that there is no Christ, neither has been, nor ever will be.

10 And I said unto him: Believest thou the scriptures? And he said, Yea.

11 And I said unto him: Then ye do not understand them; for they truly testify of Christ. Behold, I say unto you that none of the prophets have written, nor prophesied, save they have spoken concerning this Christ.

Date _____
☐ Completed

12 And this is not all—it has been made manifest unto me, for I have heard and seen; and it also has been made manifest unto me by the power of the Holy Ghost; wherefore, I know if there should be no atonement made all mankind must be lost.

13 And it came to pass that he said unto me: Show me a sign by this power of the Holy Ghost, in the which ye know so much.

14 And I said unto him: What am I that I should tempt God to show unto thee a sign in the thing which thou knowest to be true? Yet thou wilt deny it, because thou art of the devil. Nevertheless, not my will be done; but if God shall smite thee, let that be a sign unto thee that he has power, both in heaven and in earth; and also, that Christ shall come. And thy will, O Lord, be done, and not mine.

15 And it came to pass that when I, Jacob, had spoken these words, the power of the Lord came upon him, insomuch that he fell to the earth. And it came to pass that he was nourished for the space of many days.

16 And it came to pass that he said unto the people: Gather together on the morrow, for I shall die; wherefore, I desire to speak unto the people before I shall die.

17 And it came to pass that on the morrow the multitude were gathered together; and he spake plainly unto them and denied the things which he had taught them, and confessed the Christ, and the power of the Holy Ghost, and the ministering of angels.

18 And he spake plainly unto them, that he had been deceived by the power of the devil. And he spake of hell, and of eternity, and of eternal punishment.

19 And he said: I fear lest I have committed the unpardonable sin, for I have lied unto God; for I denied the Christ, and said that I believed the scriptures; and they truly testify of him. And because I have thus lied unto God I greatly fear lest my case shall be awful; but I confess unto God.

20 And it came to pass that when he had said these words he could say no more, and he gave up the ghost.

21 And when the multitude had witnessed that he spake these things as he was about to give up the ghost, they were astonished exceedingly; insomuch that the power of God came down upon them, and they were overcome that they fell to the earth.

22 Now, this thing was pleasing unto me, Jacob, for I had requested it of my Father who was in heaven; for he had heard my cry and answered my prayer.

23 And it came to pass that peace and the love of God was restored again among the people; and they searched the scriptures, and hearkened no more to the words of this wicked man.

Date _____
☐ Completed

Date _____
☐ Completed

24 And it came to pass that many means were devised to reclaim and restore the Lamanites to the knowledge of the truth; but it all was vain, for they delighted in wars and bloodshed, and they had an eternal hatred against us, their brethren. And they sought by the power of their arms to destroy us continually.

25 Wherefore, the people of Nephi did fortify against them with their arms, and with all their might, trusting in the God and rock of their salvation; wherefore, they became as yet, conquerors of their enemies.

26 And it came to pass that I, Jacob, began to be old; and the record of this people being kept on the other plates of Nephi, wherefore, I conclude this record, declaring that I have written according to the best of my knowledge, by saying that the time passed away with us, and also our lives passed away like as it were unto us a dream, we being a lonesome and a solemn people, wanderers, cast out from Jerusalem, born in tribulation, in a wilderness, and hated of our brethren, which caused wars and contentions; wherefore, we did mourn out our days.

27 And I, Jacob, saw that I must soon go down to my grave; wherefore, I said unto my son Enos: Take these plates. And I told him the things which my brother Nephi had commanded me, and he promised obedience unto the commands. And I make an end of my writing upon these plates, which writing has been small; and to the reader I bid farewell, hoping that many of my brethren may read my words. Brethren, adieu.

Date _____

☐ Completed

Enos 1

1 Behold, it came to pass that I, Enos, knowing my father that he was a just man—for he taught me in his language, and also in the nurture and admonition of the Lord—and blessed be the name of my God for it—

2 And I will tell you of the wrestle which I had before God, before I received a remission of my sins.

3 Behold, I went to hunt beasts in the forests; and the words which I had often heard my father speak concerning eternal life, and the joy of the saints, sunk deep into my heart.

4 And my soul hungered; and I kneeled down before my Maker, and I cried unto him in mighty prayer and supplication for mine own soul; and all the day long did I cry unto him; yea, and when the night came I did still raise my voice high that it reached the heavens.

5 And there came a voice unto me, saying: Enos, thy sins are forgiven thee, and thou shalt be blessed.

6 And I, Enos, knew that God could not lie; wherefore, my guilt was swept away.

7 And I said: Lord, how is it done?

8 And he said unto me: Because of thy faith in Christ, whom thou hast never before heard nor seen. And many years pass away before he shall manifest himself in the flesh; wherefore, go to, thy faith hath made thee whole.

9 Now, it came to pass that when I had heard these words I began to feel a desire for the welfare of my brethren, the Nephites; wherefore, I did pour out my whole soul unto God for them.

10 And while I was thus struggling in the spirit, behold, the voice of the Lord came into my mind again, saying: I will visit thy brethren according to their diligence in keeping my commandments. I have given unto them this land, and it is a holy land; and I curse it not save it be for the cause of iniquity; wherefore, I will visit thy brethren according as I have said; and their transgressions will I bring down with sorrow upon their own heads.

11 And after I, Enos, had heard these words, my faith began to be unshaken in the Lord; and I prayed unto him with many long strugglings for my brethren, the Lamanites.

12 And it came to pass that after I had prayed and labored with all diligence, the Lord said unto me: I will grant unto thee according to thy desires, because of thy faith.

13 And now behold, this was the desire which I desired of him—that if it should so be, that my people, the Nephites, should fall into transgression,

Date _____
☐ Completed

Date _____
☐ Completed

and by any means be destroyed, and the Lamanites should not be destroyed, that the Lord God would preserve a record of my people, the Nephites; even if it so be by the power of his holy arm, that it might be brought forth at some future day unto the Lamanites, that, perhaps, they might be brought unto salvation—

14 For at the present our strugglings were vain in restoring them to the true faith. And they swore in their wrath that, if it were possible, they would destroy our records and us, and also all the traditions of our fathers.

15 Wherefore, I knowing that the Lord God was able to preserve our records, I cried unto him continually, for he had said unto me: Whatsoever thing ye shall ask in faith, believing that ye shall receive in the name of Christ, ye shall receive it.

16 And I had faith, and I did cry unto God that he would preserve the records; and he covenanted with me that he would bring them forth unto the Lamanites in his own due time.

17 And I, Enos, knew it would be according to the covenant which he had made; wherefore my soul did rest.

18 And the Lord said unto me: Thy fathers have also required of me this thing; and it shall be done unto them according to their faith; for their faith was like unto thine.

19 And now it came to pass that I, Enos, went about among the people of Nephi, prophesying of things to come, and testifying of the things which I had heard and seen.

20 And I bear record that the people of Nephi did seek diligently to restore the Lamanites unto the true faith in God. But our labors were vain; their hatred was fixed, and they were led by their evil nature that they became wild, and ferocious, and a blood-thirsty people, full of idolatry and filthiness; feeding upon beasts of prey; dwelling in tents, and wandering about in the wilderness with a short skin girdle about their loins and their heads shaven; and their skill was in the bow, and in the cimeter, and the ax. And many of them did eat nothing save it was raw meat; and they were continually seeking to destroy us.

21 And it came to pass that the people of Nephi did till the land, and raise all manner of grain, and of fruit, and flocks of herds, and flocks of all manner of cattle of every kind, and goats, and wild goats, and also many horses.

22 And there were exceedingly many prophets among us. And the people were a stiffnecked people, hard to understand.

23 And there was nothing save it was exceeding harshness, preaching and prophesying of wars, and contentions, and destructions, and continually reminding them of death, and the duration of eternity, and the judgments

Date _____
☐ Completed

Date _____
☐ Completed

and the power of God, and all these things—stirring them up continually to keep them in the fear of the Lord. I say there was nothing short of these things, and exceedingly great plainness of speech, would keep them from going down speedily to destruction. And after this manner do I write concerning them.

24 And I saw wars between the Nephites and Lamanites in the course of my days.

25 And it came to pass that I began to be old, and an hundred and seventy and nine years had passed away from the time that our father Lehi left Jerusalem.

26 And I saw that I must soon go down to my grave, having been wrought upon by the power of God that I must preach and prophesy unto this people, and declare the word according to the truth which is in Christ. And I have declared it in all my days, and have rejoiced in it above that of the world.

27 And I soon go to the place of my rest, which is with my Redeemer; for I know that in him I shall rest. And I rejoice in the day when my mortal shall put on immortality, and shall stand before him; then shall I see his face with pleasure, and he will say unto me: Come unto me, ye blessed, there is a place prepared for you in the mansions of my Father. Amen.

Date _____

☐ Completed

Jarom

Chapter 1

Sight (Memorization) Words

done

Word Pattern

Pattern	-ore
Pattern words in scriptures	**more**
Location in chapter	Verses 2, 6, 14
Exceptions to the rule	boar, poor, floor, drawer
Other words made from this patterns not found in chapter	bore, tore, wore, score, s'more, snore, spore, store, chore, shore

Phonics Application

- *Long Vowel Sounds:* the long sound of vowels make the sound of the letter.
  - The long sound of O (example: m**o**re)
- *The Silent E rule:* when an E is at the end of a word, the E is silent and it makes the vowel to the left say its name. (When other rules apply to the word, a word that ends in E is still silent, for example: serve [see R-controlled vowels].)
- *Consonant-Vowel-Blend and Blend-Vowel-Blend:* these patterns are the merging together of sounds to make words. A blend is the combination of two (or more) consonants together. These are the blends: BL, CL, FL, GL, PL, SL, BR, CR, DR, FR, GR, PR, TR, SC, SK, SM, SN, SP, ST, SW, TW.
- *Consonant Diagraphs:* diagraphs are two letters that make one sound. The diagraphs are TH, CH, SH, WH.
- *Complex Consonants:* blends that include three consonants, two consonants that sounds like a single letter, and consonant and vowel clusters. The complex consonants are QU, TCH, CK.

Recommended (Age Appropriate) Reading Chunks

- Verses 1–4
- Verses 5–9
- Verses 10–15

Gospel Principle Review/Activity

- Why do the Nephites look forward to the coming of Christ?
- *Activity:* Find the things in this chapter that are similar to our day and things that are different.

Similar	**Different**
_____	_____
_____	_____
_____	_____

Word Patterns

_ore

Words made with –ore word pattern.
Use alphabet letters to create words.

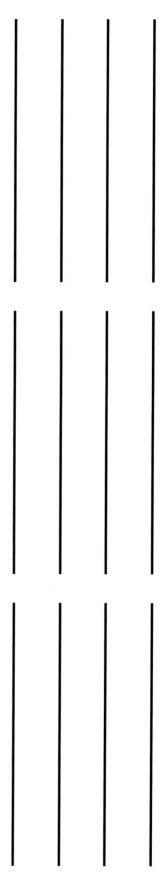

Jarom 1

1 Now behold, I, Jarom, write a few words according to the commandment of my father, Enos, that our genealogy may be kept.

2 And as these plates are small, and as these things are written for the intent of the benefit of our brethren the Lamanites, wherefore, it must needs be that I write a little; but I shall not write the things of my prophesying, nor of my revelations. For what could I write more than my fathers have written? For have not they revealed the plan of salvation? I say unto you, Yea; and this sufficeth me.

3 Behold, it is expedient that much should be done among this people, because of the hardness of their hearts, and the deafness of their ears, and the blindness of their minds, and the stiffness of their necks; nevertheless, God is exceedingly merciful unto them, and has not as yet swept them off from the face of the land.

4 And there are many among us who have many revelations, for they are not all stiffnecked. And as many as are not stiffnecked and have faith, have communion with the Holy Spirit, which maketh manifest unto the children of men, according to their faith.

5 And now, behold, two hundred years had passed away, and the people of Nephi had waxed strong in the land. They observed to keep the law of Moses and the sabbath day holy unto the Lord. And they profaned not; neither did they blaspheme. And the laws of the land were exceedingly strict.

6 And they were scattered upon much of the face of the land, and the Lamanites also. And they were exceedingly more numerous than were they of the Nephites; and they loved murder and would drink the blood of beasts.

7 And it came to pass that they came many times against us, the Nephites, to battle. But our kings and our leaders were mighty men in the faith of the Lord; and they taught the people the ways of the Lord; wherefore, we withstood the Lamanites and swept them away out of our lands, and began to fortify our cities, or whatsoever place of our inheritance.

8 And we multiplied exceedingly, and spread upon the face of the land, and became exceedingly rich in gold, and in silver, and in precious things, and in fine workmanship of wood, in buildings, and in machinery, and also in iron and copper, and brass and steel, making all manner of tools of every kind to till the ground, and weapons of war—yea, the sharp pointed arrow, and the quiver, and the dart, and the javelin, and all preparations for war.

9 And thus being prepared to meet the Lamanites, they did not prosper against us. But the word of the Lord was verified, which he spake unto our fathers, saying that: Inasmuch as ye will keep my commandments ye shall prosper in the land.

10 And it came to pass that the prophets of the Lord did threaten the people of Nephi, according to the word of God, that if they did not keep the commandments, but should fall into transgression, they should be destroyed from off the face of the land.

11 Wherefore, the prophets, and the priests, and the teachers, did labor diligently, exhorting with all long-suffering the people to diligence; teaching the law of Moses, and the intent for which it was given; persuading them to look forward unto the Messiah, and believe in him to come as though he already was. And after this manner did they teach them.

12 And it came to pass that by so doing they kept them from being destroyed upon the face of the land; for they did prick their hearts with the word, continually stirring them up unto repentance.

13 And it came to pass that two hundred and thirty and eight years had passed away—after the manner of wars, and contentions, and dissensions, for the space of much of the time.

14 And I, Jarom, do not write more, for the plates are small. But behold, my brethren, ye can go to the other plates of Nephi; for behold, upon them the records of our wars are engraven, according to the writings of the kings, or those which they caused to be written.

15 And I deliver these plates into the hands of my son Omni, that they may be kept according to the commandments of my fathers.

Date _____
☐ Completed

Omni

Chapter 1

Sight (Memorization) Words

come

Word Pattern

Pattern	-one
Pattern words in scriptures	**stone**
Location in chapter	Verse 20
Exceptions to the rule	done, gone, moan, none
Other words made from this patterns not found in chapter	alone, atone, bone, cone, hone, lone, tone, clone, scone, shone, throne

Phonics Application

- *Long Vowel Sounds:* the long sound of vowels make the sound of the letter.
  - The long sound of O (example: m**o**re)
- *The Silent E rule:* when an E is at the end of a word, the E is silent and it makes the vowel to the left say its name. (When other rules apply to the word, a word that ends in E is still silent, for example: serve [see R-controlled vowels].)
- *Consonant-Vowel-Blend and Blend-Vowel-Blend:* these patterns are the merging together of sounds to make words. A blend is the combination of two (or more) consonants together. These are the blends: BL, CL, FL, GL, PL, SL, BR, CR, DR, FR, GR, PR, TR, SC, SK, SM, SN, SP, ST, SW, TW.
- *Consonant Diagraphs:* diagraphs are two letters that make one sound. The diagraphs are TH, CH, SH, WH.
- *Complex Consonants:* blends that include three consonants, two consonants that sounds like a single letter, and consonant and vowel clusters. The complex consonants are QU, TCH, CK.

Recommended (Age Appropriate) Reading Chunks

- Verses 1–5
- Verses 6–10
- Verses 11–14
- Verses 15–19
- Verses 20–25
- Verses 26–30

Gospel Principle Review/Activity

- How many people took turns writing in this chapter?
- Is Omni a righteous man?
- *Activity:* During a Family Home Evening, pass your journal to each member of your family and have them write something about their experiences with the gospel or their testimony (similar to how the Book of Omni is written).

Word Patterns

–one

Words made with –one word pattern.
Use alphabet letters to create words.

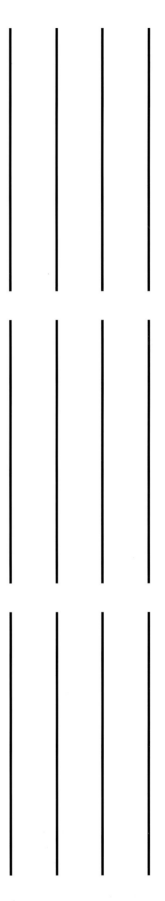

Omni 1

1 Behold, it came to pass that I, Omni, being commanded by my father, Jarom, that I should write somewhat upon these plates, to preserve our genealogy—

2 Wherefore, in my days, I would that ye should know that I fought much with the sword to preserve my people, the Nephites, from falling into the hands of their enemies, the Lamanites. But behold, I of myself am a wicked man, and I have not kept the statutes and the commandments of the Lord as I ought to have done.

3 And it came to pass that two hundred and seventy and six years had passed away, and we had many seasons of peace; and we had many seasons of serious war and bloodshed. Yea, and in fine, two hundred and eighty and two years had passed away, and I had kept these plates according to the commandments of my fathers; and I conferred them upon my son Amaron. And I make an end.

4 And now I, Amaron, write the things whatsoever I write, which are few, in the book of my father.

5 Behold, it came to pass that three hundred and twenty years had passed away, and the more wicked part of the Nephites were destroyed.

6 For the Lord would not suffer, after he had led them out of the land of Jerusalem and kept and preserved them from falling into the hands of their enemies, yea, he would not suffer that the words should not be verified, which he spake unto our fathers, saying that: Inasmuch as ye will not keep my commandments ye shall not prosper in the land.

7 Wherefore, the Lord did visit them in great judgment; nevertheless, he did spare the righteous that they should not perish, but did deliver them out of the hands of their enemies.

8 And it came to pass that I did deliver the plates unto my brother Chemish.

9 Now I, Chemish, write what few things I write, in the same book with my brother; for behold, I saw the last which he wrote, that he wrote it with his own hand; and he wrote it in the day that he delivered them unto me. And after this manner we keep the records, for it is according to the commandments of our fathers. And I make an end.

10 Behold, I, Abinadom, am the son of Chemish. Behold, it came to pass that I saw much war and contention between my people, the Nephites, and the Lamanites; and I, with my own sword, have taken the lives of many of the Lamanites in the defence of my brethren.

11 And behold, the record of this people is engraven upon plates which is had by the kings, according to the generations; and I know of no revelation

Date _____
☐ Completed

Date _____
☐ Completed

save that which has been written, neither prophecy; wherefore, that which is sufficient is written. And I make an end.

12 Behold, I am Amaleki, the son of Abinadom. Behold, I will speak unto you somewhat concerning Mosiah, who was made king over the land of Zarahemla; for behold, he being warned of the Lord that he should flee out of the land of Nephi, and as many as would hearken unto the voice of the Lord should also depart out of the land with him, into the wilderness—

13 And it came to pass that he did according as the Lord had commanded him. And they departed out of the land into the wilderness, as many as would hearken unto the voice of the Lord; and they were led by many preachings and prophesyings. And they were admonished continually by the word of God; and they were led by the power of his arm, through the wilderness until they came down into the land which is called the land of Zarahemla.

14 And they discovered a people, who were called the people of Zarahemla. Now, there was great rejoicing among the people of Zarahemla; and also Zarahemla did rejoice exceedingly, because the Lord had sent the people of Mosiah with the plates of brass which contained the record of the Jews.

15 Behold, it came to pass that Mosiah discovered that the people of Zarahemla came out from Jerusalem at the time that Zedekiah, king of Judah, was carried away captive into Babylon.

16 And they journeyed in the wilderness, and were brought by the hand of the Lord across the great waters, into the land where Mosiah discovered them; and they had dwelt there from that time forth.

17 And at the time that Mosiah discovered them, they had become exceedingly numerous. Nevertheless, they had had many wars and serious contentions, and had fallen by the sword from time to time; and their language had become corrupted; and they had brought no records with them; and they denied the being of their Creator; and Mosiah, nor the people of Mosiah, could understand them.

18 But it came to pass that Mosiah caused that they should be taught in his language. And it came to pass that after they were taught in the language of Mosiah, Zarahemla gave a genealogy of his fathers, according to his memory; and they are written, but not in these plates.

19 And it came to pass that the people of Zarahemla, and of Mosiah, did unite together; and Mosiah was appointed to be their king.

20 And it came to pass in the days of Mosiah, there was a large stone brought unto him with engravings on it; and he did interpret the engravings by the gift and power of God.

21 And they gave an account of one Coriantumr, and the slain of his

77

people. And Coriantumr was discovered by the people of Zarahemla; and he dwelt with them for the space of nine moons.

22 It also spake a few words concerning his fathers. And his first parents came out from the tower, at the time the Lord confounded the language of the people; and the severity of the Lord fell upon them according to his judgments, which are just; and their bones lay scattered in the land northward.

23 Behold, I, Amaleki, was born in the days of Mosiah; and I have lived to see his death; and Benjamin, his son, reigneth in his stead.

24 And behold, I have seen, in the days of king Benjamin, a serious war and much bloodshed between the Nephites and the Lamanites. But behold, the Nephites did obtain much advantage over them; yea, insomuch that king Benjamin did drive them out of the land of Zarahemla.

25 And it came to pass that I began to be old; and, having no seed, and knowing king Benjamin to be a just man before the Lord, wherefore, I shall deliver up these plates unto him, exhorting all men to come unto God, the Holy One of Israel, and believe in prophesying, and in revelations, and in the ministering of angels, and in the gift of speaking with tongues, and in the gift of interpreting languages, and in all things which are good; for there is nothing which is good save it comes from the Lord; and that which is evil cometh from the devil.

26 And now, my beloved brethren, I would that ye should come unto Christ, who is the Holy One of Israel, and partake of his salvation, and the power of his redemption. Yea, come unto him, and offer your whole souls as an offering unto him, and continue in fasting and praying, and endure to the end; and as the Lord liveth ye will be saved.

27 And now I would speak somewhat concerning a certain number who went up into the wilderness to return to the land of Nephi; for there was a large number who were desirous to possess the land of their inheritance.

28 Wherefore, they went up into the wilderness. And their leader being a strong and mighty man, and a stiffnecked man, wherefore he caused a contention among them; and they were all slain, save fifty, in the wilderness, and they returned again to the land of Zarahemla.

29 And it came to pass that they also took others to a considerable number, and took their journey again into the wilderness.

30 And I, Amaleki, had a brother, who also went with them; and I have not since known concerning them. And I am about to lie down in my grave; and these plates are full. And I make an end of my speaking.

Notes

Date _____
☐ Completed

Date _____
☐ Completed

Words of Mormon

1 And now I, Mormon, being about to deliver up the record which I have been making into the hands of my son Moroni, behold I have witnessed almost all the destruction of my people, the Nephites.

2 And it is many hundred years after the coming of Christ that I deliver these records into the hands of my son; and it supposeth me that he will witness the entire destruction of my people. But may God grant that he may survive them, that he may write somewhat concerning them, and somewhat concerning Christ, that perhaps some day it may profit them.

3 And now, I speak somewhat concerning that which I have written; for after I had made an abridgment from the plates of Nephi, down to the reign of this king Benjamin, of whom Amaleki spake, I searched among the records which had been delivered into my hands, and I found these plates, which contained this small account of the prophets, from Jacob down to the reign of this king Benjamin, and also many of the words of Nephi.

4 And the things which are upon these plates pleasing me, because of the prophecies of the coming of Christ; and my fathers knowing that many of them have been fulfilled; yea, and I also know that as many things as have been prophesied concerning us down to this day have been fulfilled, and as many as go beyond this day must surely come to pass—

Date _____
☐ Completed

5 Wherefore, I chose these things, to finish my record upon them, which remainder of my record I shall take from the plates of Nephi; and I cannot write the hundredth part of the things of my people.

6 But behold, I shall take these plates, which contain these prophesyings and revelations, and put them with the remainder of my record, for they are choice unto me; and I know they will be choice unto my brethren.

7 And I do this for a wise purpose; for thus it whispereth me, according to the workings of the Spirit of the Lord which is in me. And now, I do not know all things; but the Lord knoweth all things which are to come; wherefore, he worketh in me to do according to his will.

8 And my prayer to God is concerning my brethren, that they may once again come to the knowledge of God, yea, the redemption of Christ; that they may once again be a delightsome people.

9 And now I, Mormon, proceed to finish out my record, which I take from the plates of Nephi; and I make it according to the knowledge and the understanding which God has given me.

Date _____
☐ Completed

10 Wherefore, it came to pass that after Amaleki had delivered up these plates into the hands of king Benjamin, he took them and put them

with the other plates, which contained records which had been handed down by the kings, from generation to generation until the days of king Benjamin.

11 And they were handed down from king Benjamin, from generation to generation until they have fallen into my hands. And I, Mormon, pray to God that they may be preserved from this time henceforth. And I know that they will be preserved; for there are great things written upon them, out of which my people and their brethren shall be judged at the great and last day, according to the word of God which is written.

12 And now, concerning this king Benjamin—he had somewhat of contentions among his own people.

13 And it came to pass also that the armies of the Lamanites came down out of the land of Nephi, to battle against his people. But behold, king Benjamin gathered together his armies, and he did stand against them; and he did fight with the strength of his own arm, with the sword of Laban.

14 And in the strength of the Lord they did contend against their enemies, until they had slain many thousands of the Lamanites. And it came to pass that they did contend against the Lamanites until they had driven them out of all the lands of their inheritance.

15 And it came to pass that after there had been false Christs, and their mouths had been shut, and they punished according to their crimes;

16 And after there had been false prophets, and false preachers and teachers among the people, and all these having been punished according to their crimes; and after there having been much contention and many dissensions away unto the Lamanites, behold, it came to pass that king Benjamin, with the assistance of the holy prophets who were among his people—

17 For behold, king Benjamin was a holy man, and he did reign over his people in righteousness; and there were many holy men in the land, and they did speak the word of God with power and with authority; and they did use much sharpness because of the stiffneckedness of the people—

18 Wherefore, with the help of these, king Benjamin, by laboring with all the might of his body and the faculty of his whole soul, and also the prophets, did once more establish peace in the land.

Date _____
☐ Completed

Date _____
☐ Completed

Mosiah 1

1 And now there was no more contention in all the land of Zarahemla, among all the people who belonged to king Benjamin, so that king Benjamin had continual peace all the remainder of his days.

2 And it came to pass that he had three sons; and he called their names Mosiah, and Helorum, and Helaman. And he caused that they should be taught in all the language of his fathers, that thereby they might become men of understanding; and that they might know concerning the prophecies which had been spoken by the mouths of their fathers, which were delivered them by the hand of the Lord.

3 And he also taught them concerning the records which were engraven on the plated of brass, saying: My sons, I would that ye should remember that were it not for these plated, which contain these records and these commandments, we must have suffered in ignorance, even at this present time, not knowing the mysteries of God.

4 For it were not possible that our father, Lehi, could have remembered all these things, to have taught them to his children, except it were for the help of these plated; for he having been taught in the language of the Egyptians therefore he could read these engravings, and teach them to his children, that thereby they could teach them to their children, and so fulfilling the commandments of God, even down to this present time.

5 I say unto you, my sons, were it not for these things, which have been kept and preserved by the hand of God, that we might read and understand of his mysteries, and have his commandments always before our eyes, that even our fathers would have dwindled in unbelief, and we should have been like unto our brethren, the Lamanites, who know nothing concerning these things, or even do not believe them when they are taught them, because of the traditions of their fathers, which are not correct.

6 O my sons, I would that ye should remember that these sayings are true, and also that these records are true. And behold, also the plated of Nephi, which contain the records and the sayings of our fathers from the time they left Jerusalem until now, and they are true; and we can know of their surety because we have them before our eyes.

7 And now, my sons, I would that ye should remember to search them diligently, that ye may profit thereby; and I would that ye should keep the commandments of God, that ye may prosper in the land according to the promises which the Lord made unto our fathers.

8 And many more things did king Benjamin teach his sons, which are not written in this book.

Date _____
☐ Completed

Date _____
☐ Completed

9 And it came to pass that after king Benjamin had made an end of teaching his sons, that he waxed old, and he saw that he must very soon go the way of all the earth; therefore, he thought it expedient that he should confer the kingdom upon one of his sons.

10 Therefore, he had Mosiah brought before him; and these are the words which he spake unto him, saying: My son, I would that ye should make a proclamation throughout all this land among all this people, or the people of Zarahemla, and the people of Mosiah who dwell in the land, that thereby they may be gathered together; for on the morrow I shall proclaim unto this my people out of mine own mouth that thou art a king and a ruler over this people, whom the Lord our God hath given us.

11 And moreover, I shall give this people a name, that thereby they may be distinguished above all the people which the Lord God hath brought out of the land of Jerusalem; and this I do because they have been a diligent people in keeping the commandments of the Lord.

12 And I give unto them a name that never shall be blotted out, except it be through transgression.

13 Yea, and moreover I say unto you, that if this highly favored people of the Lord should fall into transgression, and become a wicked and an adulterous people, that the Lord will deliver them up, that thereby they become weak like unto their brethren; and he will no more preserve them by his matchless and marvelous power, as he has hitherto preserved our fathers.

14 For I say unto you, that if he had not extended his arm in the preservation of our fathers they must have fallen into the hands of the Lamanites, and become victims to their hatred.

15 And it came to pass that after king Benjamin had made an end of these sayings to his son, that he gave him charge concerning all the affairs of the kingdom.

16 And moreover, he also gave him charge concerning the records which were engraven on the plated of brass; and also the plated of Nephi; and also, the sword of Laban, and the ball or director, which led our fathers through the wilderness, which was prepared by the hand of the Lord that thereby they might be led, every one according to the heed and diligence which they gave unto him.

17 Therefore, as they were unfaithful they did not prosper nor progress in their journey, but were driven back, and incurred the displeasure of God upon them; and therefore they were smitten with famine and sore afflictions, to stir them up in remembrance of their duty.

18 And now, it came to pass that Mosiah went and did as his father had commanded him, and proclaimed unto all the people who were in the land of Zarahemla that thereby they might gather themselves together, to go up to the temple to hear the words which his father should speak unto them.

Date _____
☐ Completed

Date _____
☐ Completed

Mosiah 2

1 And it came to pass that after Mosiah had done as his father had commanded him, and had made a proclamation throughout all the land, that the people gathered themselves together throughout all the land, that they might go up to the temple to hear the words which king Benjamin should speak unto them.

2 And there were a great number, even so many that they did not number them; for they had multiplied exceedingly and waxed great in the land.

3 And they also took of the firstlings of their flocks, that they might offer sacrifice and burnt offerings according to the law of Moses;

4 And also that they might give thanks to the Lord their God, who had brought them out of the land of Jerusalem, and who had delivered them out of the hands of their enemies, and had appointed just men to be their teachers, and also a just man to be their king, who had established peace in the land of Zarahemla, and who had taught them to keep the commandments of God, that they might rejoice and be filled with love towards God and all men.

5 And it came to pass that when they came up to the temple, they pitched their tents round about, every man according to his family, consisting of his wife, and his sons, and his daughters, and their sons, and their daughters, from the eldest down to the youngest, every family being separate one from another.

6 And they pitched their tents round about the temple, every man having his tent with the door thereof towards the temple, that thereby they might remain in their tents and hear the words which king Benjamin should speak unto them;

7 For the multitude being so great that king Benjamin could not teach them all within the walls of the temple, therefore he caused a tower to be erected, that thereby his people might hear the words which he should speak unto them.

8 And it came to pass that he began to speak to his people from the tower; and they could not all hear his words because of the greatness of the multitude; therefore he caused that the words which he spake should be written and sent forth among those that were not under the sound of his voice, that they might also receive his words.

9 And these are the words which he spake and caused to be written, saying: My brethren, all ye that have assembled yourselves together, you that can hear my words which I shall speak unto you this day; for I have not commanded you to come up hither to trifle with the words which I shall speak, but that you should hearken unto me, and open your ears that ye may hear, and your hearts that ye may understand, and your minds that the mysteries of God may be unfolded to your view.

Date _____
☐ Completed

Date _____
☐ Completed

89

10 I have not commanded you to come up hither that ye should fear me, or that ye should think that I of myself am more than a mortal man.

11 But I am like as yourselves, subject to all manner of infirmities in body and mind; yet I have been chosen by this people, and consecrated by my father, and was suffered by the hand of the Lord that I should be a ruler and a king over this people; and have been kept and preserved by his matchless power, to serve you with all the might, mind and strength which the Lord hath granted unto me.

12 I say unto you that as I have been suffered to spend my days in your service, even up to this time, and have not sought gold nor silver nor any manner of riches of you;

13 Neither have I suffered that ye should be confined in dungeons, nor that ye should make slaves one of another, nor that ye should murder, or plunder, or steal, or commit adultery; nor even have I suffered that ye should commit any manner of wickedness, and have taught you that ye should keep the commandments of the Lord, in all things which he hath commanded you—

14 And even I, myself, have labored with mine own hands that I might serve you, and that ye should not be laden with taxes, and that there should nothing come upon you which was grievous to be borne—and of all these things which I have spoken, ye yourselves are witnesses this day.

15 Yet, my brethren, I have not done these things that I might boast, neither do I tell these things that thereby I might accuse you; but I tell you these things that ye may know that I can answer a clear conscience before God this day.

16 Behold, I say unto you that because I said unto you that I had spent my days in your service, I do not desire to boast, for I have only been in the service of God.

17 And behold, I tell you these things that ye may learn wisdom; that ye may learn that when ye are in the service of your fellow beings ye are only in the service of your God.

18 Behold, ye have called me your king; and if I, whom ye call your king, do labor to serve you, then ought not ye to labor to serve one another?

19 And behold also, if I, whom ye call your king, who has spent his days in your service, and yet has been in the service of God, do merit any thanks from you, O how you ought to thank your heavenly King!

20 I say unto you, my brethren, that if you should render all the thanks and praise which your whole soul has power to possess, to that God who has created you, and has kept and preserved you, and has caused that ye should rejoice, and has granted that ye should live in peace one with another—

21 I say unto you that if ye should serve him who has created you from the beginning, and is preserving you from day to day, by lending you breath, that ye may live and move and do according to your own will, and even

Date _____
☐ Completed

Date _____
☐ Completed

supporting you from one moment to another—I say, if ye should serve him with all your whole souls yet ye would be unprofitable servants.

22 And behold, all that he requires of you is to keep his commandments; and he has promised you that if ye would keep his commandments ye should prosper in the land; and he never doth vary from that which he hath said; therefore, if ye do keep his commandments he doth bless you and prosper you.

23 And now, in the first place, he hath created you, and granted unto you your lives, for which ye are indebted unto him.

24 And secondly, he doth require that ye should do as he hath commanded you; for which if ye do, he doth immediately bless you; and therefore he hath paid you. And ye are still indebted unto him, and are, and will be, forever and ever; therefore, of what have ye to boast?

25 And now I ask, can ye say aught of yourselves? I answer you, Nay. Ye cannot say that ye are even as much as the dust of the earth; yet ye were created of the dust of the earth; but behold, it belongeth to him who created you.

26 And I, even I, whom ye call your king, am no better than ye yourselves are; for I am also of the dust. And ye behold that I am old, and am about to yield up this mortal frame to its mother earth.

27 Therefore, as I said unto you that I had served you, walking with a clear conscience before God, even so I at this time have caused that ye should assemble yourselves together, that I might be found blameless, and that your blood should not come upon me, when I shall stand to be judged of God of the things whereof he hath commanded me concerning you.

28 I say unto you that I have caused that ye should assemble yourselves together that I might rid my garments of your blood, at this period of time when I am about to go down to my grave, that I might go down in peace, and my immortal spirit may join the choirs above in singing the praises of a just God.

29 And moreover, I say unto you that I have caused that ye should assemble yourselves together, that I might declare unto you that I can no longer be your teacher, nor your king;

30 For even at this time, my whole frame doth tremble exceedingly while attempting to speak unto you; but the Lord God doth support me, and hath suffered me that I should speak unto you, and hath commanded me that I should declare unto you this day, that my son Mosiah is a king and a ruler over you.

31 And now, my brethren, I would that ye should do as ye have hitherto done. As ye have kept my commandments, and also the commandments of my father, and have prospered, and have been kept from falling into the hands of your enemies, even so if ye shall keep the commandments of my son, or the commandments of God which shall be delivered unto

Date _____
☐ Completed

Date _____
☐ Completed

you by him, ye shall prosper in the land, and your enemies shall have no power over you.

32 But, O my people, beware lest there shall arise contentions among you, and ye list to obey the evil spirit, which was spoken of by my father Mosiah.

33 For behold, there is a wo pronounced upon him who listeth to obey that spirit; for if he listeth to obey him, and remaineth and dieth in his sins, the same drinketh damnation to his own soul; for he receiveth for his wages an everlasting punishment, having transgressed the law of God contrary to his own knowledge.

34 I say unto you, that there are not any among you, except it be your little children that have not been taught concerning these things, but what knoweth that ye are eternally indebted to your heavenly Father, to render to him all that you have and are; and also have been taught concerning the records which contain the prophecies which have been spoken by the holy prophets, even down to the time our father, Lehi, left Jerusalem;

35 And also, all that has been spoken by our fathers until now. And behold, also, they spake that which was commanded them of the Lord; therefore, they are just and true.

36 And now, I say unto you, my brethren, that after ye have known and have been taught all these things, if ye should transgress and go contrary to that which has been spoken, that ye do withdraw yourselves from the Spirit of the Lord, that it may have no place in you to guide you in wisdom's paths that ye may be blessed, prospered, and preserved—

37 I say unto you, that the man that doeth this, the same cometh out in open rebellion against God; therefore he listeth to obey the evil spirit, and becometh an enemy to all righteousness; therefore, the Lord has no place in him, for he dwelleth not in unholy temples.

38 Therefore if that man repenteth not, and remaineth and dieth an enemy to God, the demands of divine justice do awaken his immortal soul to a lively sense of his own guilt, which doth cause him to shrink from the presence of the Lord, and doth fill his breast with guilt, and pain, and anguish, which is like an unquenchable fire, whose flame ascendeth up forever and ever.

39 And now I say unto you, that mercy hath no claim on that man; therefore his final doom is to endure a never-ending torment.

40 O, all ye old men, and also ye young men, and you little children who can understand my words, for I have spoken plainly unto you that ye might understand, I pray that ye should awake to a remembrance of the awful situation of those that have fallen into transgression.

41 And moreover, I would desire that ye should consider on the blessed and happy state of those that keep the commandments of God. For behold, they are blessed in all things, both temporal and spiritual; and if they hold out faithful to the end they are received into heaven, that thereby they may dwell with God in a state of never-ending happiness. O remember, remember that these things are true; for the Lord God hath spoken it.

Date _____

☐ Completed

Date _____

☐ Completed

Mosiah 3

1 And again my brethren, I would call your attention, for I have somewhat more to speak unto you; for behold, I have things to tell you concerning that which is to come.

2 And the things which I shall tell you are made known unto me by an angel from God. And he said unto me: Awake; and I awoke, and behold he stood before me.

3 And he said unto me: Awake, and hear the words which I shall tell thee; for behold, I am come to declare unto you the glad tidings of great joy.

4 For the Lord hath heard thy prayers, and hath judged of thy righteousness, and hath sent me to declare unto thee that thou mayest rejoice; and that thou mayest declare unto thy people, that they may also be filled with joy.

5 For behold, the time cometh, and is not far distant, that with power, the Lord Omnipotent who reigneth, who was, and is from all eternity to all eternity, shall come down from heaven among the children of men, and shall dwell in a tabernacle of clay, and shall go forth amongst men, working mighty miracles, such as healing the sick, raising the dead, causing the lame to walk, the blind to receive their sight, and the deaf to hear, and curing all manner of diseases.

6 And he shall cast out devils, or the evil spirits which dwell in the hearts of the children of men.

Date _____
☐ Completed

7 And lo, he shall suffer temptations, and pain of body, hunger, thirst, and fatigue, even more than man can suffer, except it be unto death; for behold, blood cometh from every pore, so great shall be his anguish for the wickedness and the abominations of his people.

8 And he shall be called Jesus Christ, the Son of God, the Father of heaven and earth, the Creator of all things from the beginning; and his mother shall be called Mary.

9 And lo, he cometh unto his own, that salvation might come unto the children of men even through faith on his name; and even after all this they shall consider him a man, and say that he hath a devil, and shall scourge him, and shall crucify him.

10 And he shall rise the third day from the dead; and behold, he standeth to judge the world; and behold, all these things are done that a righteous judgment might come upon the children of men.

11 For behold, and also his blood atoneth for the sins of those who have fallen by the transgression of Adam, who have died not knowing the will of God concerning them, or who have ignorantly sinned.

Date _____
☐ Completed

12 But wo, wo unto him who knoweth that he rebelleth against God! For salvation cometh to none such except it be through repentance and faith on the Lord Jesus Christ.

13 And the Lord God hath sent his holy prophets among all the children of men, to declare these things to every kindred, nation, and tongue, that thereby whosoever should believe that Christ should come, the same might receive remission of their sins, and rejoice with exceedingly great joy, even as though he had already come among them.

14 Yet the Lord God saw that his people were a stiffnecked people, and he appointed unto them a law, even the law of Moses.

15 And many signs, and wonders, and types, and shadows showed he unto them, concerning his coming; and also holy prophets spake unto them concerning his coming; and yet they hardened their hearts, and understood not that the law of Moses availeth nothing except it were through the atonement of his blood.

16 And even if it were possible that little children could sin they could not be saved; but I say unto you they are blessed; for behold, as in Adam, or by nature, they fall, even so the blood of Christ atoneth for their sins.

17 And moreover, I say unto you, that there shall be no other name given nor any other way nor means whereby salvation can come unto the children of men, only in and through the name of Christ, the Lord Omnipotent.

18 For behold he judgeth, and his judgment is just; and the infant perisheth not that dieth in his infancy; but men drink damnation to their own souls except they humble themselves and become as little children, and believe that salvation was, and is, and is to come, in and through the atoning blood of Christ, the Lord Omnipotent.

19 For the natural man is an enemy to God, and has been from the fall of Adam, and will be, forever and ever, unless he yields to the enticings of the Holy Spirit, and putteth off the natural man and becometh a saint through the atonement of Christ the Lord, and becometh as a child, submissive, meek, humble, patient, full of love, willing to submit to all things which the Lord seeth fit to inflict upon him, even as a child doth submit to his father.

20 And moreover, I say unto you, that the time shall come when the knowledge of a Savior shall spread throughout every nation, kindred, tongue, and people.

21 And behold, when that time cometh, none shall be found blameless before God, except it be little children, only through repentance and faith on the name of the Lord God Omnipotent.

22 And even at this time, when thou shalt have taught thy people the things which the Lord thy God hath commanded thee, even then are

they found no more blameless in the sight of God, only according to the words which I have spoken unto thee.

23 And now I have spoken the words which the Lord God hath commanded me.

24 And thus saith the Lord: They shall stand as a bright testimony against this people, at the judgment day; whereof they shall be judged, every man according to his works, whether they be good, or whether they be evil.

25 And if they be evil they are consigned to an awful view of their own guilt and abominations, which doth cause them to shrink from the presence of the Lord into a state of misery and endless torment, from whence they can no more return; therefore they have drunk damnation to their own souls.

26 Therefore, they have drunk out of the cup of the wrath of God, which justice could no more deny unto them than it could deny that Adam should fall because of his partaking of the forbidden fruit; therefore, mercy could have claim on them no more forever.

27 And their torment is as a lake of fire and brimstone, whose flames are unquenchable, and whose smoke ascendeth up forever and ever. Thus hath the Lord commanded me. Amen.

Date _____

☐ Completed

Mosiah

Chapter 4

Sight (Memorization) Words

live

Word Pattern or Rule

Pattern or rule	-ue
Pattern words in scriptures	**due, true**
Location in chapter	Verses 12–13
Exceptions to the rule	cruel, fuel
Other words made from this patterns not found in chapter	blue, clue, cue, flue, glue, hue, sue

Phonics Application

- *Long Vowel Sounds:* the long sound of vowels make the sound of the letter.
  - The long sound of U (example: tr**ue**)
- *The Double Vowel rule:* when two vowels are together, the first vowel says its name and the second vowel is silent. (When two vowels go walking, the first one does the talking.)
- *The Silent E rule:* when an E is at the end of a word, the E is silent and it makes the vowel to the left say its name. (When other rules apply to the word, a word that ends in E is still silent, for example: serve [see R-controlled vowels].)

Recommended (Age Appropriate) Reading Chunks

- Verses 1–4
- Verses 5–8
- Verses 9–13
- Verses 14–18
- Verses 19–23
- Verses 24–27
- Verses 28–30

Gospel Principle Review/Activity

- What should we do to help the poor?
- What do we need to do to be saved?
- Why are we counseled to do all things "in wisdom and order"?
- *Activity:* Draw a picture of what you imagine this event (King Benjamin addressing his people) looked like.

Word Patterns

ue

Words made with –ue word pattern.
Use alphabet letters to create words.

Mosiah 4

1 And now, it came to pass that when king Benjamin had made an end of speaking the words which had been delivered unto him by the angel of the Lord, that he cast his eyes round about on the multitude, and behold they had fallen to the earth, for the fear of the Lord had come upon them.

2 And they had viewed themselves in their own carnal state, even less than the dust of the earth. And they all cried aloud with one voice, saying: O have mercy, and apply the atoning blood of Christ that we may receive forgiveness of our sins, and our hearts may be purified; for we believe in Jesus Christ, the Son of God, who created heaven and earth, and all things; who shall come down among the children of men.

3 And it came to pass that after they had spoken these words the Spirit of the Lord came upon them, and they were filled with joy, having received a remission of their sins, and having peace of conscience, because of the exceeding faith which they had in Jesus Christ who should come, according to the words which king Benjamin had spoken unto them.

4 And king Benjamin again opened his mouth and began to speak unto them, saying: My friends and my brethren, my kindred and my people, I would again call your attention, that ye may hear and understand the remainder of my words which I shall speak unto you.

---

5 For behold, if the knowledge of the goodness of God at this time has awakened you to a sense of your nothingness, and your worthless and fallen state—

6 I say unto you, if ye have come to a knowledge of the goodness of God, and his matchless power, and his wisdom, and his patience, and his long-suffering towards the children of men; and also, the atonement which has been prepared from the foundation of the world, that thereby salvation might come to him that should put his trust in the Lord, and should be diligent in keeping his commandments, and continue in the faith even unto the end of his life, I mean the life of the mortal body—

7 I say, that this is the man who receiveth salvation, through the atonement which was prepared from the foundation of the world for all mankind, which ever were since the fall of Adam, or who are, or who ever shall be, even unto the end of the world.

8 And this is the means whereby salvation cometh. And there is none other salvation save this which hath been spoken of; neither are there any conditions whereby man can be saved except the conditions which I have told you.

---

9 Believe in God; believe that he is, and that he created all things, both in heaven and in earth; believe that he has all wisdom, and all power, both in heaven and in earth; believe that man doth not comprehend all the things which the Lord can comprehend.

10 And again, believe that ye must repent of your sins and forsake them, and

Date _____
☐ Completed

Date _____
☐ Completed

humble yourselves before God; and ask in sincerity of heart that he would forgive you; and now, if you believe all these things see that ye do them.

11 And again I say unto you as I have said before, that as ye have come to the knowledge of the glory of God, or if ye have known of his goodness and have tasted of his love, and have received a remission of your sins, which causeth such exceedingly great joy in your souls, even so I would that ye should remember, and always retain in remembrance, the greatness of God, and your own nothingness, and his goodness and long-suffering towards you, unworthy creatures, and humble yourselves even in the depths of humility, calling on the name of the Lord daily, and standing steadfastly in the faith of that which is to come, which was spoken by the mouth of the angel.

12 And behold, I say unto you that if ye do this ye shall always rejoice, and be filled with the love of God, and always retain a remission of your sins; and ye shall grow in the knowledge of the glory of him that created you, or in the knowledge of that which is just and true.

13 And ye will not have a mind to injure one another, but to live peaceably, and to render to every man according to that which is his due.

14 And ye will not suffer your children that they go hungry, or naked; neither will ye suffer that they transgress the laws of God, and fight and quarrel one with another, and serve the devil, who is the master of sin, or who is the evil spirit which hath been spoken of by our fathers, he being an enemy to all righteousness.

15 But ye will teach them to walk in the ways of truth and soberness; ye will teach them to love one another, and to serve one another.

16 And also, ye yourselves will succor those that stand in need of your succor; ye will administer of your substance unto him that standeth in need; and ye will not suffer that the beggar putteth up his petition to you in vain, and turn him out to perish.

17 Perhaps thou shalt say: The man has brought upon himself his misery; therefore I will stay my hand, and will not give unto him of my food, nor impart unto him of my substance that he may not suffer, for his punishments are just—

18 But I say unto you, O man, whosoever doeth this the same hath great cause to repent; and except he repenteth of that which he hath done he perisheth forever, and hath no interest in the kingdom of God.

19 For behold, are we not all beggars? Do we not all depend upon the same Being, even God, for all the substance which we have, for both food and raiment, and for gold, and for silver, and for all the riches which we have of every kind?

20 And behold, even at this time, ye have been calling on his name, and begging for a remission of your sins. And has he suffered that ye have begged in vain? Nay; he has poured out his Spirit upon you, and has caused that your

Date _____
☐ Completed

Date _____
☐ Completed

hearts should be filled with joy, and has caused that your mouths should be stopped that ye could not find utterance, so exceedingly great was your joy.

21 And now, if God, who has created you, on whom you are dependent for your lives and for all that ye have and are, doth grant unto you whatsoever ye ask that is right, in faith, believing that ye shall receive, O then, how ye ought to impart of the substance that ye have one to another.

22 And if ye judge the man who putteth up his petition to you for your substance that he perish not, and condemn him, how much more just will be your condemnation for withholding your substance, which doth not belong to you but to God, to whom also your life belongeth; and yet ye put up no petition, nor repent of the thing which thou hast done.

23 I say unto you, wo be unto that man, for his substance shall perish with him; and now, I say these things unto those who are rich as pertaining to the things of this world.

24 And again, I say unto the poor, ye who have not and yet have sufficient, that ye remain from day to day; I mean all you who deny the beggar, because ye have not; I would that ye say in your hearts that: I give not because I have not, but if I had I would give.

25 And now, if ye say this in your hearts ye remain guiltless, otherwise ye are condemned; and your condemnation is just for ye covet that which ye have not received.

26 And now, for the sake of these things which I have spoken unto you—that is, for the sake of retaining a remission of your sins from day to day, that ye may walk guiltless before God—I would that ye should impart of your substance to the poor, every man according to that which he hath, such as feeding the hungry, clothing the naked, visiting the sick and administering to their relief, both spiritually and temporally, according to their wants.

27 And see that all these things are done in wisdom and order; for it is not requisite that a man should run faster than he has strength. And again, it is expedient that he should be diligent, that thereby he might win the prize; therefore, all things must be done in order.

28 And I would that ye should remember, that whosoever among you borroweth of his neighbor should return the thing that he borroweth, according as he doth agree, or else thou shalt commit sin; and perhaps thou shalt cause thy neighbor to commit sin also.

29 And finally, I cannot tell you all the things whereby ye may commit sin; for there are divers ways and means, even so many that I cannot number them.

30 But this much I can tell you, that if ye do not watch yourselves, and your thoughts, and your words, and your deeds, and observe the commandments of God, and continue in the faith of what ye have heard concerning the coming of our Lord, even unto the end of your lives, ye must perish. And now, O man, remember, and perish not.

Date _____
☐ Completed

Date _____
☐ Completed

Date _____
☐ Completed

Mosiah 5

1 And now, it came to pass that when king Benjamin had thus spoken to his people, he sent among them, desiring to know of his people if they believed the words which he had spoken unto them.

2 And they all cried with one voice, saying: Yea, we believe all the words which thou hast spoken unto us; and also, we know of their surety and truth, because of the Spirit of the Lord Omnipotent, which has wrought a mighty change in us, or in our hearts, that we have no more disposition to do evil, but to do good continually.

3 And we, ourselves, also, through the infinite goodness of God, and the manifestations of his Spirit, have great views of that which is to come; and were it expedient, we could prophesy of all things.

4 And it is the faith which we have had on the things which our king has spoken unto us that has brought us to this great knowledge, whereby we do rejoice with such exceedingly great joy.

5 And we are willing to enter into a covenant with our God to do his will, and to be obedient to his commandments in all things that he shall command us, all the remainder of our days, that we may not bring upon ourselves a never–ending torment, as has been spoken by the angel, that we may not drink out of the cup of the wrath of God.

6 And now, these are the words which king Benjamin desired of them; and therefore he said unto them: Ye have spoken the words that I desired; and the covenant which ye have made is a righteous covenant.

7 And now, because of the covenant which ye have made ye shall be called the children of Christ, his sons, and his daughters; for behold, this day he hath spiritually begotten you; for ye say that your hearts are changed through faith on his name; therefore, ye are born of him and have become his sons and his daughters.

8 And under this head ye are made free, and there is no other head whereby ye can be made free. There is no other name given whereby salvation cometh; therefore, I would that ye should take upon you the name of Christ, all you that have entered into the covenant with God that ye should be obedient unto the end of your lives.

9 And it shall come to pass that whosoever doeth this shall be found at the right hand of God, for he shall know the name by which he is called; for he shall be called by the name of Christ.

10 And now it shall come to pass, that whosoever shall not take upon him the name of Christ must be called by some other name; therefore, he findeth himself on the left hand of God.

11 And I would that ye should remember also, that this is the name that

Date _____
☐ Completed

Date _____
☐ Completed

I said I should give unto you that never should be blotted out, except it be through transgression; therefore, take heed that ye do not transgress, that the name be not blotted out of your hearts.

12 I say unto you, I would that ye should remember to retain the name written always in your hearts, that ye are not found on the left hand of God, but that ye hear and know the voice by which ye shall be called, and also, the name by which he shall call you.

13 For how knoweth a man the master whom he has not served, and who is a stranger unto him, and is far from the thoughts and intents of his heart?

14 And again, doth a man take an ass which belongeth to his neighbor, and keep him? I say unto you, Nay; he will not even suffer that he shall feed among his flocks, but will drive him away, and cast him out. I say unto you, that even so shall it be among you if ye know not the name by which ye are called.

15 Therefore, I would that ye should be steadfast and immovable, always abounding in good works, that Christ, the Lord God Omnipotent, may seal you his, that you may be brought to heaven, that ye may have everlasting salvation and eternal life, through the wisdom, and power, and justice, and mercy of him who created all things, in heaven and in earth, who is God above all. Amen.

Date _____

☐ Completed

Mosiah 6

1 And now, king Benjamin thought it was expedient, after having finished speaking to the people, that he should take the names of all those who had entered into a covenant with God to keep his commandments.

2 And it came to pass that there was not one soul, except it were little children, but who had entered into the covenant and had taken upon them the name of Christ.

3 And again, it came to pass that when king Benjamin had made an end of all these things, and had consecrated his son Mosiah to be a ruler and a king over his people, and had given him all the charges concerning the kingdom, and also had appointed priests to teach the people, that thereby they might hear and know the commandments of God, and to stir them up in remembrance of the oath which they had made, he dismissed the multitude, and they returned, every one, according to their families, to their own houses.

4 And Mosiah began to reign in his father's stead. And he began to reign in the thirtieth year of his age, making in the whole, about four hundred and seventy-six years from the time that Lehi left Jerusalem.

5 And king Benjamin lived three years and he died.

6 And it came to pass that king Mosiah did walk in the ways of the Lord, and did observe his judgments and his statutes, and did keep his commandments in all things whatsoever he commanded him.

7 And king Mosiah did cause his people that they should till the earth. And he also, himself, did till the earth, that thereby he might not become burdensome to his people, that he might do according to that which his father had done in all things. And there was no contention among all his people for the space of three years.

Date _____

☐ Completed

Mosiah

Chapter 7

Sight (Memorization) Words

else	**bold**

Word Pattern or Rule

Pattern or Rule	-ie
Pattern words in scriptures	(none)
Location in chapter	(none)
Exceptions to the rule	views, chief, field, brief, fiend, grief, grieve, liege, niece, piece, priest, shield, shriek, siege, thief, yield
Other words made from this patterns not found in chapter	lie, lied (-ied found in Alma 18), pie, tie, die, cried, tried, dried

Phonics Application

- *Long Vowel Sounds:* the long sound of vowels make the sound of the letter.
  - The long sound of I (example: p**ie**)
- *The Double Vowel rule:* when two vowels are together, the first vowel says its name and the second vowel is silent. (When two vowels go walking, the first one does the talking.)
- *The Silent E rule:* when an E is at the end of a word, the E is silent and it makes the vowel to the left say its name. (When other rules apply to the word, a word that ends in E is still silent, for example: serve [see R-controlled vowels].)

Recommended (Age Appropriate) Reading Chunks

- Verses 1–7
- Verses 8–12
- Verses 13–16
- Verses 17–20
- Verses 21–25
- Verses 26–33

Gospel Principle Review/Activity

- Why were Ammon and his brethren spared and not killed?
- What is the problem with King Limhi's people? Is King Limhi a good man?
- *Activity:* It was hard for Mosiah's people to know where to go without any map or hints. Create a treasure map and have a sibling or friend follow it to the treasure.

Word Patterns

_ie_

Words made with –ie word pattern.
Use alphabet letters to create words.

Mosiah 7

1 And now, it came to pass that after king Mosiah had had continual peace for the space of three years, he was desirous to know concerning the people who went up to dwell in the land of Lehi-Nephi, or in the city of Lehi-Nephi; for his people had heard nothing from them from the time they left the land of Zarahemla; therefore, they wearied him with their teasings.

2 And it came to pass that king Mosiah granted that sixteen of their strong men might go up to the land of Lehi-Nephi, to inquire concerning their brethren.

3 And it came to pass that on the morrow they started to go up, having with them one Ammon, he being a strong and mighty man, and a descendant of Zarahemla; and he was also their leader.

4 And now, they knew not the course they should travel in the wilderness to go up to the land of Lehi-Nephi; therefore they wandered many days in the wilderness, even forty days did they wander.

5 And when they had wandered forty days they came to a hill, which is north of the land of Shilom, and there they pitched their tents.

6 And Ammon took three of his brethren, and their names were Amaleki, Helem, and Hem, and they went down into the land of Nephi.

7 And behold, they met the king of the people who were in the land of Nephi, and in the land of Shilom; and they were surrounded by the king's guard, and were taken, and were bound, and were committed to prison.

Date _____

☐ Completed

8 And it came to pass when they had been in prison two days they were again brought before the king, and their bands were loosed; and they stood before the king, and were permitted, or rather commanded, that they should answer the questions which he should ask them.

9 And he said unto them: Behold, I am Limhi, the son of Noah, who was the son of Zeniff, who came up out of the land of Zarahemla to inherit this land, which was the land of their fathers, who was made a king by the voice of the people.

10 And now, I desire to know the cause whereby ye were so bold as to come near the walls of the city, when I, myself, was with my guards without the gate?

11 And now, for this cause have I suffered that ye should be preserved, that I might inquire of you, or else I should have caused that my guards should have put you to death. Ye are permitted to speak.

12 And now, when Ammon saw that he was permitted to speak, he went forth and bowed himself before the king; and rising again he said: O king, I am very thankful before God this day that I am yet alive, and am permitted to speak; and I will endeavor to speak with boldness;

Date _____

☐ Completed

13 For I am assured that if ye had known me ye would not have suffered that I should have worn these bands. For I am Ammon, and am a descendant of Zarahemla, and have come up out of the land of Zarahemla to inquire concerning our brethren, whom Zeniff brought up out of that land.

14 And now, it came to pass that after Limhi had heard the words of Ammon, he was exceedingly glad, and said: Now, I know of a surety that my brethren who were in the land of Zarahemla are yet alive. And now, I will rejoice; and on the morrow I will cause that my people shall rejoice also.

15 For behold, we are in bondage to the Lamanites, and are taxed with a tax which is grievous to be borne. And now, behold, our brethren will deliver us out of our bondage, or out of the hands of the Lamanites, and we will be their slaves; for it is better that we be slaves to the Nephites than to pay tribute to the king of the Lamanites.

16 And now, king Limhi commanded his guards that they should no more bind Ammon nor his brethren, but caused that they should go to the hill which was north of Shilom, and bring their brethren into the city, that thereby they might eat, and drink, and rest themselves from the labors of their journey; for they had suffered many things; they had suffered hunger, thirst, and fatigue.

17 And now, it came to pass on the morrow that king Limhi sent a proclamation among all his people, that thereby they might gather themselves together to the temple, to hear the words which he should speak unto them.

18 And it came to pass that when they had gathered themselves together that he spake unto them in this wise, saying: O ye, my people, lift up your heads and be comforted; for behold, the time is at hand, or is not far distant, when we shall no longer be in subjection to our enemies, notwithstanding our many strugglings, which have been in vain; yet I trust there remaineth an effectual struggle to be made.

19 Therefore, lift up your heads, and rejoice, and put your trust in God, in that God who was the God of Abraham, and Isaac, and Jacob; and also, that God who brought the children of Israel out of the land of Egypt, and caused that they should walk through the Red Sea on dry ground, and fed them with manna that they might not perish in the wilderness; and many more things did he do for them.

20 And again, that same God has brought our fathers out of the land of Jerusalem, and has kept and preserved his people even until now; and behold, it is because of our iniquities and abominations that he has brought us into bondage.

21 And ye all are witnesses this day, that Zeniff, who was made king over this people, he being over–zealous to inherit the land of his fathers, therefore being deceived by the cunning and craftiness of king Laman,

Date _____
☐ Completed

Date _____
☐ Completed

who having entered into a treaty with king Zeniff, and having yielded up into his hands the possessions of a part of the land, or even the city of Lehi-Nephi, and the city of Shilom; and the land round about—

22 And all this he did, for the sole purpose of bringing this people into subjection or into bondage. And behold, we at this time do pay tribute to the king of the Lamanites, to the amount of one half of our corn, and our barley, and even all our grain of every kind, and one half of the increase of our flocks and our herds; and even one half of all we have or possess the king of the Lamanites doth exact of us, or our lives.

23 And now, is not this grievous to be borne? And is not this, our affliction, great? Now behold, how great reason we have to mourn.

24 Yea, I say unto you, great are the reasons which we have to mourn; for behold how many of our brethren have been slain, and their blood has been spilt in vain, and all because of iniquity.

25 For if this people had not fallen into transgression the Lord would not have suffered that this great evil should come upon them. But behold, they would not hearken unto his words; but there arose contentions among them, even so much that they did shed blood among themselves.

26 And a prophet of the Lord have they slain; yea, a chosen man of God, who told them of their wickedness and abominations, and prophesied of many things which are to come, yea, even the coming of Christ.

27 And because he said unto them that Christ was the God, the Father of all things, and said that he should take upon him the image of man, and it should be the image after which man was created in the beginning; or in other words, he said that man was created after the image of God, and that God should come down among the children of men, and take upon him flesh and blood, and go forth upon the face of the earth—

28 And now, because he said this, they did put him to death; and many more things did they do which brought down the wrath of God upon them. Therefore, who wondereth that they are in bondage, and that they are smitten with sore afflictions?

29 For behold, the Lord hath said: I will not succor my people in the day of their transgression; but I will hedge up their ways that they prosper not; and their doings shall be as a stumbling block before them.

30 And again, he saith: If my people shall sow filthiness they shall reap the chaff thereof in the whirlwind; and the effect thereof is poison.

31 And again he saith: If my people shall sow filthiness they shall reap the east wind, which bringeth immediate destruction.

32 And now, behold, the promise of the Lord is fulfilled, and ye are smitten and afflicted.

33 But if ye will turn to the Lord with full purpose of heart, and put your trust in him, and serve him with all diligence of mind, if ye do this, he will, according to his own will and pleasure, deliver you out of bondage.

Date _____

☐ Completed

Date _____

☐ Completed

Mosiah 8

1 And it came to pass that after king Limhi had made an end of speaking to his people, for he spake many things unto them and only a few of them have I written in this book, he told his people all the things concerning their brethren who were in the land of Zarahemla.

2 And he caused that Ammon should stand up before the multitude, and rehearse unto them all that had happened unto their brethren from the time that Zeniff went up out of the land even until the time that he himself came up out of the land.

3 And he also rehearsed unto them the last words which king Benjamin had taught them, and explained them to the people of king Limhi, so that they might understand all the words which he spake.

4 And it came to pass that after he had done all this, that king Limhi dismissed the multitude, and caused that they should return every one unto his own house.

5 And it came to pass that he caused that the plates which contained the record of his people from the time that they left the land of Zarahemla, should be brought before Ammon, that he might read them.

6 Now, as soon as Ammon had read the record, the king inquired of him to know if he could interpret languages, and Ammon told him that he could not.

Date _____

☐ Completed

7 And the king said unto him: Being grieved for the afflictions of my people, I caused that forty and three of my people should take a journey into the wilderness, that thereby they might find the land of Zarahemla, that we might appeal unto our brethren to deliver us out of bondage.

8 And they were lost in the wilderness for the space of many days, yet they were diligent, and found not the land of Zarahemla but returned to this land, having traveled in a land among many waters, having discovered a land which was covered with bones of men, and of beasts, and was also covered with ruins of buildings of every kind, having discovered a land which had been peopled with a people who were as numerous as the hosts of Israel.

9 And for a testimony that the things that they had said are true they have brought twenty–four plates which are filled with engravings, and they are of pure gold.

10 And behold, also, they have brought breastplates, which are large, and they are of brass and of copper, and are perfectly sound.

11 And again, they have brought swords, the hilts thereof have perished, and the blades thereof were cankered with rust; and there is no one in the land that is able to interpret the language or the engravings that are on the plates. Therefore I said unto thee: Canst thou translate?

Date _____

☐ Completed

12 And I say unto thee again: Knowest thou of any one that can translate? For I am desirous that these records should be translated into our language; for, perhaps, they will give us a knowledge of a remnant of the people who have been destroyed, from whence these records came; or, perhaps, they will give us a knowledge of this very people who have been destroyed; and I am desirous to know the cause of their destruction.

13 Now Ammon said unto him: I can assuredly tell thee, O king, of a man that can translate the records; for he has wherewith that he can look, and translate all records that are of ancient date; and it is a gift from God. And the things are called interpreters, and no man can look in them except he be commanded, lest he should look for that he ought not and he should perish. And whosoever is commanded to look in them, the same is called seer.

14 And behold, the king of the people who are in the land of Zarahemla is the man that is commanded to do these things, and who has this high gift from God.

15 And the king said that a seer is greater than a prophet.

16 And Ammon said that a seer is a revelator and a prophet also; and a gift which is greater can no man have, except he should possess the power of God, which no man can; yet a man may have great power given him from God.

---

17 But a seer can know of things which are past, and also of things which are to come, and by them shall all things be revealed, or, rather, shall secret things be made manifest, and hidden things shall come to light, and things which are not known shall be made known by them, and also things shall be made known by them which otherwise could not be known.

18 Thus God has provided a means that man, through faith, might work mighty miracles; therefore he becometh a great benefit to his fellow beings.

19 And now, when Ammon had made an end of speaking these words the king rejoiced exceedingly, and gave thanks to God, saying: Doubtless a great mystery is contained within these plates, and these interpreters were doubtless prepared for the purpose of unfolding all such mysteries to the children of men.

20 O how marvelous are the works of the Lord, and how long doth he suffer with his people; yea, and how blind and impenetrable are the understandings of the children of men; for they will not seek wisdom, neither do they desire that she should rule over them!

21 Yea, they are as a wild flock which fleeth from the shepherd, and scattereth, and are driven, and are devoured by the beasts of the forest.

Date _____
☐ Completed

Date _____
☐ Completed

Mosiah 9

1 I, Zeniff, having been taught in all the language of the Nephites, and having had a knowledge of the land of Nephi, or of the land of our fathers' first inheritance, and having been sent as a spy among the Lamanites that I might spy out their forces, that our army might come upon them and destroy them—but when I saw that which was good among them I was desirous that they should not be destroyed.

2 Therefore, I contended with my brethren in the wilderness, for I would that our ruler should make a treaty with them; but he being an austere and a blood-thirsty man commanded that I should be slain; but I was rescued by the shedding of much blood; for father fought against father, and brother against brother, until the greater number of our army was destroyed in the wilderness; and we returned, those of us that were spared, to the land of Zarahemla, to relate that tale to their wives and their children.

3 And yet, I being over–zealous to inherit the land of our fathers, collected as many as were desirous to go up to possess the land, and started again on our journey into the wilderness to go up to the land; but we were smitten with famine and sore afflictions; for we were slow to remember the Lord our God.

4 Nevertheless, after many days' wandering in the wilderness we pitched our tents in the place where our brethren were slain, which was near to the land of our fathers.

5 And it came to pass that I went again with four of my men into the city, in unto the king, that I might know of the disposition of the king, and that I might know if I might go in with my people and possess the land in peace.

6 And I went in unto the king, and he covenanted with me that I might possess the land of Lehi-Nephi, and the land of Shilom.

7 And he also commanded that his people should depart out of the land, and I and my people went into the land that we might possess it.

8 And we began to build buildings, and to repair the walls of the city, yea, even the walls of the city of Lehi-Nephi, and the city of Shilom.

9 And we began to till the ground, yea, even with all manner of seeds, with seeds of corn, and of wheat, and of barley, and with neas, and with sheum, and with seeds of all manner of fruits; and we did begin to multiply and prosper in the land.

10 Now it was the cunning and the craftiness of king Laman, to bring my people into bondage, that he yielded up the land that we might possess it.

Date _____
☐ Completed

Date _____
☐ Completed

11 Therefore it came to pass, that after we had dwelt in the land for the space of twelve years that king Laman began to grow uneasy, lest by any means my people should wax strong in the land, and that they could not overpower them and bring them into bondage.

12 Now they were a lazy and an idolatrous people; therefore they were desirous to bring us into bondage, that they might glut themselves with the labors of our hands; yea, that they might feast themselves upon the flocks of our fields.

13 Therefore it came to pass that king Laman began to stir up his people that they should contend with my people; therefore there began to be wars and contentions in the land.

14 For, in the thirteenth year of my reign in the land of Nephi, away on the south of the land of Shilom, when my people were watering and feeding their flocks, and tilling their lands, a numerous host of Lamanites came upon them and began to slay them, and to take off their flocks, and the corn of their fields.

15 Yea, and it came to pass that they fled, all that were not overtaken, even into the city of Nephi, and did call upon me for protection.

16 And it came to pass that I did arm them with bows, and with arrows, with swords, and with cimeters, and with clubs, and with slings, and with all manner of weapons which we could invent, and I and my people did go forth against the Lamanites to battle.

17 Yea, in the strength of the Lord did we go forth to battle against the Lamanites; for I and my people did cry mightily to the Lord that he would deliver us out of the hands of our enemies, for we were awakened to a remembrance of the deliverance of our fathers.

18 And God did hear our cries and did answer our prayers; and we did go forth in his might; yea, we did go forth against the Lamanites, and in one day and a night we did slay three thousand and forty–three; we did slay them even until we had driven them out of our land.

19 And I, myself, with mine own hands, did help to bury their dead. And behold, to our great sorrow and lamentation, two hundred and seventy–nine of our brethren were slain.

Date _____
☐ Completed

Date _____
☐ Completed

Mosiah 10

1 And it came to pass that we again began to establish the kingdom and we again began to possess the land in peace. And I caused that there should be weapons of war made of every kind, that thereby I might have weapons for my people against the time the Lamanites should come up again to war against my people.

2 And I set guards round about the land, that the Lamanites might not come upon us again unawares and destroy us; and thus I did guard my people and my flocks, and keep them from falling into the hands of our enemies.

3 And it came to pass that we did inherit the land of our fathers for many years, yea, for the space of twenty and two years.

4 And I did cause that the men should till the ground, and raise all manner of grain and all manner of fruit of every kind.

5 And I did cause that the women should spin, and toil, and work, and work all manner of fine linen, yea, and cloth of every kind, that we might clothe our nakedness; and thus we did prosper in the land—thus we did have continual peace in the land for the space of twenty and two years.

Date _____
☐ Completed

6 And it came to pass that king Laman died, and his son began to reign in his stead. And he began to stir his people up in rebellion against my people; therefore they began to prepare for war, and to come up to battle against my people.

7 But I had sent my spies out round about the land of Shemlon, that I might discover their preparations, that I might guard against them, that they might not come upon my people and destroy them.

8 And it came to pass that they came up upon the north of the land of Shilom, with their numerous hosts, men armed with bows, and with arrows, and with swords, and with cimeters, and with stones, and with slings; and they had their heads shaved that they were naked; and they were girded with a leathern girdle about their loins.

9 And it came to pass that I caused that the women and children of my people should be hid in the wilderness; and I also caused that all my old men that could bear arms, and also all my young men that were able to bear arms, should gather themselves together to go to battle against the Lamanites; and I did place them in their ranks, every man according to his age.

10 And it came to pass that we did go up to battle against the Lamanites; and I, even I, in my old age, did go up to battle against the Lamanites. And it came to pass that we did go up in the strength of the Lord to battle.

Date _____
☐ Completed

11 Now, the Lamanites knew nothing concerning the Lord, nor the strength of the Lord, therefore they depended upon their own strength. Yet they were a strong people, as to the strength of men.

12 They were a wild, and ferocious, and a blood-thirsty people, believing in the tradition of their fathers, which is this—Believing that they were driven out of the land of Jerusalem because of the iniquities of their fathers, and that they were wronged in the wilderness by their brethren, and they were also wronged while crossing the sea;

13 And again, that they were wronged while in the land of their first inheritance, after they had crossed the sea, and all this because that Nephi was more faithful in keeping the commandments of the Lord—therefore he was favored of the Lord, for the Lord heard his prayers and answered them, and he took the lead of their journey in the wilderness.

14 And his brethren were wroth with him because they understood not the dealings of the Lord; they were also wroth with him upon the waters because they hardened their hearts against the Lord.

15 And again, they were wroth with him when they had arrived in the promised land, because they said that he had taken the ruling of the people out of their hands; and they sought to kill him.

16 And again, they were wroth with him because he departed into the wilderness as the Lord had commanded him, and took the records which were engraven on the plates of brass, for they said that he robbed them.

17 And thus they have taught their children that they should hate them, and that they should murder them, and that they should rob and plunder them, and do all they could to destroy them; therefore they have an eternal hatred towards the children of Nephi.

18 For this very cause has king Laman, by his cunning, and lying craftiness, and his fair promises, deceived me, that I have brought this my people up into this land, that they may destroy them; yea, and we have suffered these many years in the land.

19 And now I, Zeniff, after having told all these things unto my people concerning the Lamanites, I did stimulate them to go to battle with their might, putting their trust in the Lord; therefore, we did contend with them, face to face.

20 And it came to pass that we did drive them again out of our land; and we slew them with a great slaughter, even so many that we did not number them.

21 And it came to pass that we returned again to our own land, and my people again began to tend their flocks, and to till their ground.

22 And now I, being old, did confer the kingdom upon one of my sons; therefore, I say no more. And may the Lord bless my people. Amen.

Date _____
☐ Completed

Date _____
☐ Completed

Mosiah 11

1 And now it came to pass that Zeniff conferred the kingdom upon Noah, one of his sons; therefore Noah began to reign in his stead; and he did not walk in the ways of his father.

2 For behold, he did not keep the commandments of God, but he did walk after the desires of his own heart. And he had many wives and concubines. And he did cause his people to commit sin, and do that which was abominable in the sight of the Lord. Yea, and they did commit whoredoms and all manner of wickedness.

3 And he laid a tax of one fifth part of all they possessed, a fifth part of their gold and of their silver, and a fifth part of their ziff, and of their copper, and of their brass and their iron; and a fifth part of their fatlings; and also a fifth part of all their grain.

4 And all this did he take to support himself, and his wives and his concubines; and also his priests, and their wives and their concubines; thus he had changed the affairs of the kingdom.

5 For he put down all the priests that had been consecrated by his father, and consecrated new ones in their stead, such as were lifted up in the pride of their hearts.

Date _____

☐ Completed

6 Yea, and thus they were supported in their laziness, and in their idolatry, and in their whoredoms, by the taxes which king Noah had put upon his people; thus did the people labor exceedingly to support iniquity.

7 Yea, and they also became idolatrous, because they were deceived by the vain and flattering words of the king and priests; for they did speak flattering things unto them.

8 And it came to pass that king Noah built many elegant and spacious buildings; and he ornamented them with fine work of wood, and of all manner of precious things, of gold, and of silver, and of iron, and of brass, and of ziff, and of copper;

9 And he also built him a spacious palace, and a throne in the midst thereof, all of which was of fine wood and was ornamented with gold and silver and with precious things.

10 And he also caused that his workmen should work all manner of fine work within the walls of the temple, of fine wood, and of copper, and of brass.

11 And the seats which were set apart for the high priests, which were above all the other seats, he did ornament with pure gold; and he caused a breastwork to be built before them, that they might rest their bodies and their arms upon while they should speak lying and vain words to his people.

Date _____

☐ Completed

12 And it came to pass that he built a tower near the temple; yea, a

very high tower, even so high that he could stand upon the top thereof and overlook the land of Shilom, and also the land of Shemlon, which was possessed by the Lamanites; and he could even look over all the land round about.

13 And it came to pass that he caused many buildings to be built in the land Shilom; and he caused a great tower to be built on the hill north of the land Shilom, which had been a resort for the children of Nephi at the time they fled out of the land; and thus he did do with the riches which he obtained by the taxation of his people.

14 And it came to pass that he placed his heart upon his riches, and he spent his time in riotous living with his wives and his concubines; and so did also his priests spend their time with harlots.

15 And it came to pass that he planted vineyards round about in the land; and he built wine–presses, and made wine in abundance; and therefore he became a wine–bibber, and also his people.

16 And it came to pass that the Lamanites began to come in upon his people, upon small numbers, and to slay them in their fields, and while they were tending their flocks.

17 And king Noah sent guards round about the land to keep them off; but he did not send a sufficient number, and the Lamanites came upon them and killed them, and drove many of their flocks out of the land; thus the Lamanites began to destroy them, and to exercise their hatred upon them.

18 And it came to pass that king Noah sent his armies against them, and they were driven back, or they drove them back for a time; therefore, they returned rejoicing in their spoil.

19 And now, because of this great victory they were lifted up in the pride of their hearts; they did boast in their own strength, saying that their fifty could stand against thousands of the Lamanites; and thus they did boast, and did delight in blood, and the shedding of the blood of their brethren, and this because of the wickedness of their king and priests.

20 And it came to pass that there was a man among them whose name was Abinadi; and he went forth among them, and began to prophesy, saying: Behold, thus saith the Lord, and thus hath he commanded me, saying, Go forth, and say unto this people, thus saith the Lord—Wo be unto this people, for I have seen their abominations, and their wickedness, and their whoredoms; and except they repent I will visit them in mine anger.

21 And except they repent and turn to the Lord their God, behold, I will deliver them into the hands of their enemies; yea, and they shall be brought into bondage; and they shall be afflicted by the hand of their enemies.

22 And it shall come to pass that they shall know that I am the Lord their God, and am a jealous God, visiting the iniquities of my people.

23 And it shall come to pass that except this people repent and turn unto the Lord their God, they shall be brought into bondage; and none shall deliver them, except it be the Lord the Almighty God.

24 Yea, and it shall come to pass that when they shall cry unto me I will be slow to hear their cries; yea, and I will suffer them that they be smitten by their enemies.

25 And except they repent in sackcloth and ashes, and cry mightily to the Lord their God, I will not hear their prayers, neither will I deliver them out of their afflictions; and thus saith the Lord, and thus hath he commanded me.

26 Now it came to pass that when Abinadi had spoken these words unto them they were wroth with him, and sought to take away his life; but the Lord delivered him out of their hands.

27 Now when king Noah had heard of the words which Abinadi had spoken unto the people, he was also wroth; and he said: Who is Abinadi, that I and my people should be judged of him, or who is the Lord, that shall bring upon my people such great affliction?

28 I command you to bring Abinadi hither, that I may slay him, for he has said these things that he might stir up my people to anger one with another, and to raise contentions among my people; therefore I will slay him.

29 Now the eyes of the people were blinded; therefore they hardened their hearts against the words of Abinadi, and they sought from that time forward to take him. And king Noah hardened his heart against the word of the Lord, and he did not repent of his evil doings.

Date ——————
☐ Completed

Mosiah

Chapter 12

Sight (Memorization) Words

Zion

Word Pattern or Rule

Pattern or Rule	-ar
Pattern words in scriptures	**are, arm, garment**
Location in chapter	Verses 10, 24
Other words made from this patterns not found in chapter	arch, art, bar, barb, barge, bark, car, card, cart, carve, charm, chart, dark, dart, far, harm, hard, harp, impart, jar, large, lark, mark, march, marvel, park, part, scar, scarf, shark, sharp, smart, snarl, spark, star, start, starve, tar, tart, yard, yarn

Phonics Application

- *R-Controlled Vowel Patterns:* vowels that are followed by an R are influenced by the R sound.
  - The R-controlled vowel sound of A (example: c**ar**)
- *The Silent E rule:* when an E is at the end of a word, the E is silent and it makes the vowel to the left say its name. (When other rules apply to the word, a word that ends in E is still silent, for example: serve [see R-controlled vowels].)

Recommended (Age Appropriate) Reading Chunks

- Verses 1–4
- Verses 5–10
- Verses 11–16
- Verses 17–24
- Verses 25–29
- Verses 30–37

Gospel Principle Review/Activity

- Why is Abinadi put in prison?
- Abinadi begins to teach the Ten Commandments. What are the Ten Commandments? (Refer to Exodus 20.)
- *Activity:* Many animals are mentioned in this chapter. Search for the animals and look for the reason they are mentioned.

Word Patterns

ar

Words made with –ar word patterns.
Use alphabet letters to create words.

Mosiah 12

1 And it came to pass that after the space of two years that Abinadi came among them in disguise, that they knew him not, and began to prophesy among them, saying: Thus has the Lord commanded me, saying— Abinadi, go and prophesy unto this my people, for they have hardened their hearts against my words; they have repented not of their evil doings; therefore, I will visit them in my anger, yea, in my fierce anger will I visit them in their iniquities and abominations.

2 Yea, wo be unto this generation! And the Lord said unto me: Stretch forth thy hand and prophesy, saying: Thus saith the Lord, it shall come to pass that this generation, because of their iniquities, shall be brought into bondage, and shall be smitten on the cheek; yea, and shall be driven by men, and shall be slain; and the vultures of the air, and the dogs, yea, and the wild beasts, shall devour their flesh.

3 And it shall come to pass that the life of king Noah shall be valued even as a garment in a hot furnace; for he shall know that I am the Lord.

4 And it shall come to pass that I will smite this my people with sore afflictions, yea, with famine and with pestilence; and I will cause that they shall howl all the day long.

5 Yea, and I will cause that they shall have burdens lashed upon their backs; and they shall be driven before like a dumb ass.

6 And it shall come to pass that I will send forth hail among them, and it shall smite them; and they shall also be smitten with the east wind; and insects shall pester their land also, and devour their grain.

7 And they shall be smitten with a great pestilence—and all this will I do because of their iniquities and abominations.

8 And it shall come to pass that except they repent I will utterly destroy them from off the face of the earth; yet they shall leave a record behind them, and I will preserve them for other nations which shall possess the land; yea, even this will I do that I may discover the abominations of this people to other nations. And many things did Abinadi prophesy against this people.

9 And it came to pass that they were angry with him; and they took him and carried him bound before the king, and said unto the king: Behold, we have brought a man before thee who has prophesied evil concerning thy people, and saith that God will destroy them.

10 And he also prophesieth evil concerning thy life, and saith that thy life shall be as a garment in a furnace of fire.

11 And again, he saith that thou shalt be as a stalk, even as a dry stalk of the field, which is run over by the beasts and trodden under foot.

Date _____
☐ Completed

Date _____
☐ Completed

12 And again, he saith thou shalt be as the blossoms of a thistle, which, when it is fully ripe, if the wind bloweth, it is driven forth upon the face of the land. And he pretendeth the Lord hath spoken it. And he saith all this shall come upon thee except thou repent, and this because of thine iniquities.

13 And now, O king, what great evil hast thou done, or what great sins have thy people committed, that we should be condemned of God or judged of this man?

14 And now, O king, behold, we are guiltless, and thou, O king, hast not sinned; therefore, this man has lied concerning you, and he has prophesied in vain.

15 And behold, we are strong, we shall not come into bondage, or be taken captive by our enemies; yea, and thou hast prospered in the land, and thou shalt also prosper.

16 Behold, here is the man, we deliver him into thy hands; thou mayest do with him as seemeth thee good.

17 And it came to pass that king Noah caused that Abinadi should be cast into prison; and he commanded that the priests should gather themselves together that he might hold a council with them what he should do with him.

18 And it came to pass that they said unto the king: Bring him hither that we may question him; and the king commanded that he should be brought before them.

19 And they began to question him, that they might cross him, that thereby they might have wherewith to accuse him; but he answered them boldly, and withstood all their questions, yea, to their astonishment; for he did withstand them in all their questions, and did confound them in all their words.

20 And it came to pass that one of them said unto him: What meaneth the words which are written, and which have been taught by our fathers, saying:

21 How beautiful upon the mountains are the feet of him that bringeth good tidings; that publisheth peace; that bringeth good tidings of good; that publisheth salvation; that saith unto Zion, Thy God reigneth;

22 Thy watchmen shall lift up the voice; with the voice together shall they sing; for they shall see eye to eye when the Lord shall bring again Zion;

23 Break forth into joy; sing together ye waste places of Jerusalem; for the Lord hath comforted his people, he hath redeemed Jerusalem;

24 The Lord hath made bare his holy arm in the eyes of all the nations, and all the ends of the earth shall see the salvation of our God?

25 And now Abinadi said unto them: Are you priests, and pretend to

Date _____
☐ Completed

Date _____
☐ Completed

teach this people, and to understand the spirit of prophesying, and yet desire to know of me what these things mean?

26 I say unto you, wo be unto you for perverting the ways of the Lord! For if ye understand these things ye have not taught them; therefore, ye have perverted the ways of the Lord.

27 Ye have not applied your hearts to understanding; therefore, ye have not been wise. Therefore, what teach ye this people?

28 And they said: We teach the law of Moses.

29 And again he said unto them: If ye teach the law of Moses why do ye not keep it? Why do ye set your hearts upon riches? Why do ye commit whoredoms and spend your strength with harlots, yea, and cause this people to commit sin, that the Lord has cause to send me to prophesy against this people, yea, even a great evil against this people?

30 Know ye not that I speak the truth? Yea, ye know that I speak the truth; and you ought to tremble before God.

31 And it shall come to pass that ye shall be smitten for your iniquities, for ye have said that ye teach the law of Moses. And what know ye concerning the law of Moses? Doth salvation come by the law of Moses? What say ye?

32 And they answered and said that salvation did come by the law of Moses.

33 But now Abinadi said unto them: I know if ye keep the commandments of God ye shall be saved; yea, if ye keep the commandments which the Lord delivered unto Moses in the mount of Sinai, saying:

34 I am the Lord thy God, who hath brought thee out of the land of Egypt, out of the house of bondage.

35 Thou shalt have no other God before me.

36 Thou shalt not make unto thee any graven image, or any likeness of any thing in heaven above, or things which are in the earth beneath.

37 Now Abinadi said unto them, Have ye done all this? I say unto you, Nay, ye have not. And have ye taught this people that they should do all these things? I say unto you, Nay, ye have not.

Date _____
☐ Completed

Date _____
☐ Completed

Mosiah 13

1 And now when the king had heard these words, he said unto his priests: Away with this fellow, and slay him; for what have we to do with him, for he is mad.

2 And they stood forth and attempted to lay their hands on him; but he withstood them, and said unto them:

3 Touch me not, for God shall smite you if ye lay your hands upon me, for I have not delivered the message which the Lord sent me to deliver; neither have I told you that which ye requested that I should tell; therefore, God will not suffer that I shall be destroyed at this time.

4 But I must fulfil the commandments wherewith God has commanded me; and because I have told you the truth ye are angry with me. And again, because I have spoken the word of God ye have judged me that I am mad.

5 Now it came to pass after Abinadi had spoken these words that the people of king Noah durst not lay their hands on him, for the Spirit of the Lord was upon him; and his face shone with exceeding luster, even as Moses' did while in the mount of Sinai, while speaking with the Lord.

6 And he spake with power and authority from God; and he continued his words, saying:

Date _____
☐ Completed

7 Ye see that ye have not power to slay me, therefore I finish my message. Yea, and I perceive that it cuts you to your hearts because I tell you the truth concerning your iniquities.

8 Yea, and my words fill you with wonder and amazement, and with anger.

9 But I finish my message; and then it matters not whither I go, if it so be that I am saved.

10 But this much I tell you, what you do with me, after this, shall be as a type and a shadow of things which are to come.

11 And now I read unto you the remainder of the commandments of God, for I perceive that they are not written in your hearts; I perceive that ye have studied and taught iniquity the most part of your lives.

12 And now, ye remember that I said unto you: Thou shall not make unto thee any graven image, or any likeness of things which are in heaven above, or which are in the earth beneath, or which are in the water under the earth.

13 And again: Thou shalt not bow down thyself unto them, nor serve them; for I the Lord thy God am a jealous God, visiting the iniquities of the fathers upon the children, unto the third and fourth generations of them that hate me;

14 And showing mercy unto thousands of them that love me and keep my commandments.

Date _____
☐ Completed

15 Thou shalt not take the name of the Lord thy God in vain; for the Lord will not hold him guiltless that taketh his name in vain.

16 Remember the sabbath day, to keep it holy.

17 Six days shalt thou labor, and do all thy work;

18 But the seventh day, the sabbath of the Lord thy God, thou shalt not do any work, thou, nor thy son, nor thy daughter, thy man–servant, nor thy maid–servant, nor thy cattle, nor thy stranger that is within thy gates;

19 For in six days the Lord made heaven and earth, and the sea, and all that in them is; wherefore the Lord blessed the sabbath day, and hallowed it.

20 Honor thy father and thy mother, that thy days may be long upon the land which the Lord thy God giveth thee.

21 Thou shalt not kill.

22 Thou shalt not commit adultery. Thou shalt not steal.

23 Thou shalt not bear false witness against thy neighbor.

24 Thou shalt not covet thy neighbor's house, thou shalt not covet thy neighbor's wife, nor his man–servant, nor his maid–servant, nor his ox, nor his ass, nor anything that is thy neighbor's.

25 And it came to pass that after Abinadi had made an end of these sayings that he said unto them: Have ye taught this people that they should observe to do all these things for to keep these commandments?

26 I say unto you, Nay; for if ye had, the Lord would not have caused me to come forth and to prophesy evil concerning this people.

27 And now ye have said that salvation cometh by the law of Moses. I say unto you that it is expedient that ye should keep the law of Moses as yet; but I say unto you, that the time shall come when it shall no more be expedient to keep the law of Moses.

28 And moreover, I say unto you, that salvation doth not come by the law alone; and were it not for the atonement, which God himself shall make for the sins and iniquities of his people, that they must unavoidably perish, notwithstanding the law of Moses.

29 And now I say unto you that it was expedient that there should be a law given to the children of Israel, yea, even a very strict law; for they were a stiffnecked people, quick to do iniquity, and slow to remember the Lord their God;

30 Therefore there was a law given them, yea, a law of performances and of ordinances, a law which they were to observe strictly from day to day, to keep them in remembrance of God and their duty towards him.

31 But behold, I say unto you, that all these things were types of things to come.

32 And now, did they understand the law? I say unto you, Nay, they did not all understand the law; and this because of the hardness of their

Date _____
☐ Completed

Date _____
☐ Completed

hearts; for they understood not that there could not any man be saved except it were through the redemption of God.

33 For behold, did not Moses prophesy unto them concerning the coming of the Messiah, and that God should redeem his people? Yea, and even all the prophets who have prophesied ever since the world began—have they not spoken more or less concerning these things?

34 Have they not said that God himself should come down among the children of men, and take upon him the form of man, and go forth in mighty power upon the face of the earth?

35 Yea, and have they not said also that he should bring to pass the resurrection of the dead, and that he, himself, should be oppressed and afflicted?

Date _____

☐ Completed

Mosiah

Chapter 14

Sight (Memorization) Words

has

(Note: the s/z rule is explained in Alma 44.)

Word Pattern or Rule

Pattern or Rule	-or
Pattern words in scriptures	**borne, for, form, Lord, nor**
Location in chapter	Verses 1–2, 4–6, 8, 10–12
Exceptions to the rule	word, work
Other words made from this patterns not found in chapter	border, cord, cork, corn, correct, corrupt, force, ford, forest, forge, fork, fort, forth, gorge, glory, horn, horse, morning, north, or, poor, pork, porch, port, scorch, scorn, short, sort, sport, stork, storm, support, sworn, thorn, torment, torn, worn

Phonics Application

- *R-Controlled Vowel Patterns:* vowels that are followed by an R are influenced by the R sound.
  - The R-controlled vowel sound of U (example: b**ur**n)
- *The Silent E rule:* when an E is at the end of a word, the E is silent and it makes the vowel to the left say its name. (When other rules apply to the word, a word that ends in E is still silent, for example: serve [see R-controlled vowels].)

Recommended (Age Appropriate) Reading Chunks

- Verses 1–6
- Verses 7–12

Gospel Principle Review/Activity

- Isaiah is talking about Christ. What are some things that he says Christ will do for us?
- How does it make you feel for Christ when you read about the way people have treated Him?
- *Activity:* The Lord is compared to a "tender plant and as a root out of dry ground." Plant a seed (either in a garden or a pot) and watch the seed grow. See how this scripture about the Lord applies to the plant. Ask yourself these questions as it grows:
  - Can the plant you planted grow in dry ground?
  - What makes a plant tender?

Word Patterns

Or ___

Words made with –or word patterns.
Use alphabet letters to create words.

Mosiah 14

1 Yea, even doth not Isaiah say: Who hath believed our report, and to whom is the arm of the Lord revealed?

2 For he shall grow up before him as a tender plant, and as a root out of dry ground; he hath no form nor comeliness; and when we shall see him there is no beauty that we should desire him.

3 He is despised and rejected of men; a man of sorrows, and acquainted with grief; and we hid as it were our faces from him; he was despised, and we esteemed him not.

4 Surely he has borne our griefs, and carried our sorrows; yet we did esteem him stricken, smitten of God, and afflicted.

5 But he was wounded for our transgressions, he was bruised for our iniquities; the chastisement of our peace was upon him; and with his stripes we are healed.

6 All we, like sheep, have gone astray; we have turned every one to his own way; and the Lord hath laid on him the iniquities of us all.

7 He was oppressed, and he was afflicted, yet he opened not his mouth; he is brought as a lamb to the slaughter, and as a sheep before her shearers is dumb so he opened not his mouth.

8 He was taken from prison and from judgment; and who shall declare his generation? For he was cut off out of the land of the living; for the transgressions of my people was he stricken.

9 And he made his grave with the wicked, and with the rich in his death; because he had done no evil, neither was any deceit in his mouth.

10 Yet it pleased the Lord to bruise him; he hath put him to grief; when thou shalt make his soul an offering for sin he shall see his seed, he shall prolong his days, and the pleasure of the Lord shall prosper in his hand.

11 He shall see the travail of his soul, and shall be satisfied; by his knowledge shall my righteous servant justify many; for he shall bear their iniquities.

12 Therefore will I divide him a portion with the great, and he shall divide the spoil with the strong; because he hath poured out his soul unto death; and he was numbered with the transgressors; and he bore the sins of many, and made intercession for the transgressors.

Date _____
☐ Completed

Date _____
☐ Completed

Mosiah 15

1 And now Abinadi said unto them: I would that ye should understand that God himself shall come down among the children of men, and shall redeem his people.

2 And because he dwelleth in flesh he shall be called the Son of God, and having subjected the flesh to the will of the Father, being the Father and the Son—

3 The Father, because he was conceived by the power of God; and the Son, because of the flesh; thus becoming the Father and Son—

4 And they are one God, yea, the very Eternal Father of heaven and of earth.

5 And thus the flesh becoming subject to the Spirit, or the Son to the Father, being one God, suffereth temptation, and yieldeth not to the temptation, but suffereth himself to be mocked, and scourged, and cast out, and disowned by his people.

6 And after all this, after working many mighty miracles among the children of men, he shall be led, yea, even as Isaiah said, as a sheep before the shearer is dumb, so he opened not his mouth.

7 Yea, even so he shall be led, crucified, and slain, the flesh becoming subject even unto death, the will of the Son being swallowed up in the will of the Father.

8 And thus God breaketh the bands of death, having gained the victory over death; giving the Son power to make intercession for the children of men—

9 Having ascended into heaven, having the bowels of mercy; being filled with compassion towards the children of men; standing betwixt them and justice; having broken the bands of death, taken upon himself their iniquity and their transgressions, having redeemed them, and satisfied the demands of justice.

10 And now I say unto you, who shall declare his generation? Behold, I say unto you, that when his soul has been made an offering for sin he shall see his seed. And now what say ye? And who shall be his seed?

11 Behold I say unto you, that whosoever has heard the words of the prophets, yea, all the holy prophets who have prophesied concerning the coming of the Lord—I say unto you, that all those who have hearkened unto their words, and believed that the Lord would redeem his people, and have looked forward to that day for a remission of their sins, I say unto you, that these are his seed, or they are the heirs of the kingdom of God.

12 For these are they whose sins he has borne; these are they for whom he has died, to redeem them from their transgressions. And now, are they not his seed?

13 Yea, and are not the prophets, every one that has opened his mouth to prophesy, that has not fallen into transgression, I mean all the holy prophets ever since the world began? I say unto you that they are his seed.

14 And these are they who have published peace, who have brought good tidings of good, who have published salvation; and said unto Zion: Thy God reigneth!

15 And O how beautiful upon the mountains were their feet!

16 And again, how beautiful upon the mountains are the feet of those that are still publishing peace!

17 And again, how beautiful upon the mountains are the feet of those who shall hereafter publish peace, yea, from this time henceforth and forever!

18 And behold, I say unto you, this is not all. For O how beautiful upon the mountains are the feet of him that bringeth good tidings, that is the founder of peace, yea, even the Lord, who has redeemed his people; yea, him who has granted salvation unto his people;

19 For were it not for the redemption which he hath made for his people, which was prepared from the foundation of the world, I say unto you, were it not for this, all mankind must have perished.

---

20 But behold, the bands of death shall be broken, and the Son reigneth, and hath power over the dead; therefore, he bringeth to pass the resurrection of the dead.

21 And there cometh a resurrection, even a first resurrection; yea, even a resurrection of those that have been, and who are, and who shall be, even until the resurrection of Christ—for so shall he be called.

22 And now, the resurrection of all the prophets, and all those that have believed in their words, or all those that have kept the commandments of God, shall come forth in the first resurrection; therefore, they are the first resurrection.

23 They are raised to dwell with God who has redeemed them; thus they have eternal life through Christ, who has broken the bands of death.

24 And these are those who have part in the first resurrection; and these are they that have died before Christ came, in their ignorance, not having salvation declared unto them. And thus the Lord bringeth about the restoration of these; and they have a part in the first resurrection, or have eternal life, being redeemed by the Lord.

25 And little children also have eternal life.

---

26 But behold, and fear, and tremble before God, for ye ought to tremble; for the Lord redeemeth none such that rebel against him and die in their sins; yea, even all those that have perished in their sins ever since the world began, that have wilfully rebelled against God, that have known the commandments of God, and would not keep them; these are they that

Date _____
☐ Completed

Date _____
☐ Completed

have no part in the first resurrection.

27 Therefore ought ye not to tremble? For salvation cometh to none such; for the Lord hath redeemed none such; yea, neither can the Lord redeem such; for he cannot deny himself; for he cannot deny justice when it has its claim.

28 And now I say unto you that the time shall come that the salvation of the Lord shall be declared to every nation, kindred, tongue, and people.

29 Yea, Lord, thy watchmen shall lift up their voice; with the voice together shall they sing; for they shall see eye to eye, when the Lord shall bring again Zion.

30 Break forth into joy, sing together, ye waste places of Jerusalem; for the Lord hath comforted his people, he hath redeemed Jerusalem.

31 The Lord hath made bare his holy arm in the eyes of all the nations; and all the ends of the earth shall see the salvation of our God.

Date _____

☐ Completed

Mosiah

Chapter 16

Sight (Memorization) Words

father

Word Pattern or Rule

Pattern or Rule	-gn, -mb
Pattern words in scriptures	**gnash**
Location in chapter	Verse 2
Exceptions to the rule	(none listed)
Other words made from this patterns not found in chapter	-gn (gnarl, gnat, gnaw, gnome, reign) -mb (bomb, climb, comb, crumb, dumb, jamb, lamb, limb, numb, plumb, thumb, tomb, womb)

Phonics Application

- *Complex Consonants:* blends that include three consonants, two consonants that sounds like a single letter, and consonant and vowel clusters. The complex consonants are QU, TCH, CK.
  - Silent Consonant: GN—the G is silent (example: **gn**at)
  - Silent Consonant: MB—the B is silent (example: co**mb**)

Recommended (Age Appropriate) Reading Chunks

- Verses 1–6
- Verses 7–15

Gospel Principle Review/Activity

- How does God redeem men from their lost and fallen state?
- What is resurrection?
- *Activity:* What does it mean to repent? *Repent* means to change things in our life so that we can be more like God. Sin is something that all of us struggle with different ways. Try an experiment. Carry around a backpack for a given time. Over the course of that time, add more things to the backpack. At the end of the time given, ask the student how it feels to have so much weight. Have someone else unzip the bag and take everything out. How does the backpack feel now?
  - How does this relate to repentance?
  - Teach how repentance is done.

Word Patterns

gn   mb

Words made with –gn, –mb word patterns.
Use alphabet letters to create words.

Mosiah 16

1 And now, it came to pass that after Abinadi had spoken these words he stretched forth his hand and said: The time shall come when all shall see the salvation of the Lord; when every nation, kindred, tongue, and people shall see eye to eye and shall confess before God that his judgments are just.

2 And then shall the wicked be cast out, and they shall have cause to howl, and weep, and wail, and gnash their teeth; and this because they would not hearken unto the voice of the Lord; therefore the Lord redeemeth them not.

3 For they are carnal and devilish, and the devil has power over them; yea, even that old serpent that did beguile our first parents, which was the cause of their fall; which was the cause of all mankind becoming carnal, sensual, devilish, knowing evil from good, subjecting themselves to the devil.

4 Thus all mankind were lost; and behold, they would have been endlessly lost were it not that God redeemed his people from their lost and fallen state.

5 But remember that he that persists in his own carnal nature, and goes on in the ways of sin and rebellion against God, remaineth in his fallen state and the devil hath all power over him. Therefore, he is as though there was no redemption made, being an enemy to God; and also is the devil an enemy to God.

6 And now if Christ had not come into the world, speaking of things to come as though they had already come, there could have been no redemption.

7 And if Christ had not risen from the dead, or have broken the bands of death that the grave should have no victory, and that death should have no sting, there could have been no resurrection.

8 But there is a resurrection, therefore the grave hath no victory, and the sting of death is swallowed up in Christ.

9 He is the light and the life of the world; yea, a light that is endless, that can never be darkened; yea, and also a life which is endless, that there can be no more death.

10 Even this mortal shall put on immortality, and this corruption shall put on incorruption, and shall be brought to stand before the bar of God, to be judged of him according to their works whether they be good or whether they be evil—

11 If they be good, to the resurrection of endless life and happiness; and if they be evil, to the resurrection of endless damnation, being delivered up to the devil, who hath subjected them, which is damnation—

12 Having gone according to their own carnal wills and desires; having

never called upon the Lord while the arms of mercy were extended towards them; for the arms of mercy were extended towards them, and they would not; they being warned of their iniquities and yet they would not depart from them; and they were commanded to repent and yet they would not repent.

13 And now, ought ye not to tremble and repent of your sins, and remember that only in and through Christ ye can be saved?

14 Therefore, if ye teach the law of Moses, also teach that it is a shadow of those things which are to come—

15 Teach them that redemption cometh through Christ the Lord, who is the very Eternal Father. Amen.

Notes

Date _____
☐ Completed

Mosiah

Chapter 17

Sight (Memorization) Words

been

Word Pattern or Rule

Pattern or Rule	-kn, -wr
Pattern words in scriptures	**wroth, write,** **knew** (starting in Alma 1, per –ew rule)
Location in chapter	Verses 2–4
Exceptions to the rule	(none)
Other words made from this patterns not found in chapter	-kn (knack, knave, knead, knee, kneel, knelt, knife, knight, knit, knob, knock, knot, know, known) -wr (wrap, wrath, wreath, wreck, wren, wrench, wrest, wring, wrist, write, wrong, wrote, wrung, wry)

Phonics Application

* *Complex Consonants:* blends that include three consonants, two consonants that sounds like a single letter, and consonant and vowel clusters. The complex consonants are QU, TCH, CK.
  * Silent Consonant: K—the K is silent (example: **kn**ot)
  * Silent Consonant: WR—the W is silent (example: **wr**ap)

Recommended (Age Appropriate) Reading Chunks

* Verses 1–7
* Verses 8–13
* Verses 14–20

Gospel Principle Review/Activity

* Who was Alma? What position did he hold in King Noah's kingdom?
* How does Abinadi die and how does he say that King Noah will die?
* *Activity:* Abinadi died because he was preaching the truth and the people didn't want to hear about it. Can you think of other people who have died that way? What blessings are in store for them?

People who have died for their faith:

_____   _____

_____   _____

Blessings: _____   _____

_____   _____

Word Patterns

___ kn ___

wr ___

Words made with –kn, –wr word patterns.
Use alphabet letters to create words.

Mosiah 17

1 And now it came to pass that when Abinadi had finished these sayings, that the king commanded that the priests should take him and cause that he should be put to death.

2 But there was one among them whose name was Alma, he also being a descendant of Nephi. And he was a young man, and he believed the words which Abinadi had spoken, for he knew concerning the iniquity which Abinadi had testified against them; therefore he began to plead with the king that he would not be angry with Abinadi, but suffer that he might depart in peace.

3 But the king was more wroth, and caused that Alma should be cast out from among them, and sent his servants after him that they might slay him.

4 But he fled from before them and hid himself that they found him not. And he being concealed for many days did write all the words which Abinadi had spoken.

5 And it came to pass that the king caused that his guards should surround Abinadi and take him; and they bound him and cast him into prison.

6 And after three days, having counseled with his priests, he caused that he should again be brought before him.

7 And he said unto him: Abinadi, we have found an accusation against thee, and thou art worthy of death.

8 For thou hast said that God himself should come down among the children of men; and now, for this cause thou shalt be put to death unless thou wilt recall all the words which thou hast spoken evil concerning me and my people.

9 Now Abinadi said unto him: I say unto you, I will not recall the words which I have spoken unto you concerning this people, for they are true; and that ye may know of their surety I have suffered myself that I have fallen into your hands.

10 Yea, and I will suffer even until death, and I will not recall my words, and they shall stand as a testimony against you. And if ye slay me ye will shed innocent blood, and this shall also stand as a testimony against you at the last day.

11 And now king Noah was about to release him, for he feared his word; for he feared that the judgments of God would come upon him.

12 But the priests lifted up their voices against him, and began to accuse him, saying: He has reviled the king. Therefore the king was stirred up in anger against him, and he delivered him up that he might be slain.

13 And it came to pass that they took him and bound him, and scourged his skin with faggots, yea, even unto death.

14 And now when the flames began to scorch him, he cried unto them, saying:

15 Behold, even as ye have done unto me, so shall it come to pass that thy seed shall cause that many shall suffer the pains that I do suffer, even the pains of death by fire; and this because they believe in the salvation of the Lord their God.

16 And it will come to pass that ye shall be afflicted with all manner of diseases because of your iniquities.

17 Yea, and ye shall be smitten on every hand, and shall be driven and scattered to and fro, even as a wild flock is driven by wild and ferocious beasts.

18 And in that day ye shall be hunted, and ye shall be taken by the hand of your enemies, and then ye shall suffer, as I suffer, the pains of death by fire.

19 Thus God executeth vengeance upon those that destroy his people. O God, receive my soul.

20 And now, when Abinadi had said these words, he fell, having suffered death by fire; yea, having been put to death because he would not deny the commandments of God, having sealed the truth of his words by his death.

Date _____

☐ Completed

157

Mosiah

Chapter 18

Sight (Memorization) Words

both

Word Pattern or Rule

Pattern or Rule	-ch, -tch
Pattern words in scriptures	**preach, teach, which, church, watch**
Location in chapter	Verses 2–4, 7, 17–20, 22, 25–27, 32
Exceptions to the rule	(none listed)
Other words made from this patterns not found in chapter	-ch (beach, beech, coach, couch, peach, poach, pouch, reach, roach, teach, bench, birch, branch, bunch, church, cinch, crunch, drench, finch, gulch, hunch, launch, lunch, march, mulch, munch, perch, pinch, porch, punch, ranch, scorch, scrunch, search, starch, torch, trench, wrench -tch(batch, blotch, botch, catch, clutch, crutch, ditch, fetch, hatch, hitch, hutch, latch, match, notch, patch, pitch, scratch, sketch, snatch, stitch, switch, thatch, twitch, witch

Phonics Application

- *Complex Consonants:* blends that include three consonants, two consonants that sounds like a single letter, and consonant and vowel clusters. The complex consonants are QU, TCH, CK.
  - *Sound alike final consonant sounds:* CH and TCH these blends make the same sound (example: **ch**at and i**tch**).

Recommended (Age Appropriate) Reading Chunks

- Verses 1–6
- Verses 7–11
- Verses 12–16
- Verses 17–22
- Verses 23–28
- Verses 29–35

Gospel Principle Review/Activity

- Why was Alma hiding?
- What special thing happened at the Waters of Mormon? What do you think the Waters of Mormon looked like?
- *Activity:* Talk to someone who has been baptized. Have him or her share pictures and memories of what it felt like and how he or she decided to be baptized.

Word Patterns

ch ___

tch ___

Words made with –kch, –tch word patterns.
Use alphabet letters to create words.

Mosiah 18

1 And now, it came to pass that Alma, who had fled from the servants of king Noah, repented of his sins and iniquities, and went about privately among the people, and began to teach the words of Abinadi—

2 Yea, concerning that which was to come, and also concerning the resurrection of the dead, and the redemption of the people, which was to be brought to pass through the power, and sufferings, and death of Christ, and his resurrection and ascension into heaven.

3 And as many as would hear his word he did teach. And he taught them privately, that it might not come to the knowledge of the king. And many did believe his words.

4 And it came to pass that as many as did believe him did go forth to a place which was called Mormon, having received its name from the king, being in the borders of the land having been infested, by times or at seasons, by wild beasts.

5 Now, there was in Mormon a fountain of pure water, and Alma resorted thither, there being near the water a thicket of small trees, where he did hide himself in the daytime from the searches of the king.

6 And it came to pass that as many as believed him went thither to hear his words.

Date _____
☐ Completed

7 And it came to pass after many days there were a goodly number gathered together at the place of Mormon, to hear the words of Alma. Yea, all were gathered together that believed on his word, to hear him. And he did teach them, and did preach unto them repentance, and redemption, and faith on the Lord.

8 And it came to pass that he said unto them: Behold, here are the waters of Mormon (for thus were they called) and now, as ye are desirous to come into the fold of God, and to be called his people, and are willing to bear one another's burdens, that they may be light;

9 Yea, and are willing to mourn with those that mourn; yea, and comfort those that stand in need of comfort, and to stand as witnesses of God at all times and in all things, and in all places that ye may be in, even until death, that ye may be redeemed of God, and be numbered with those of the first resurrection, that ye may have eternal life—

10 Now I say unto you, if this be the desire of your hearts, what have you against being baptized in the name of the Lord, as a witness before him that ye have entered into a covenant with him, that ye will serve him and keep his commandments, that he may pour out his Spirit more abundantly upon you?

11 And now when the people had heard these words, they clapped their hands for joy, and exclaimed: This is the desire of our hearts.

Date _____
☐ Completed

12 And now it came to pass that Alma took Helam, he being one of the first, and went and stood forth in the water, and cried, saying: O Lord, pour out thy Spirit upon thy servant, that he may do this work with holiness of heart.

13 And when he had said these words, the Spirit of the Lord was upon him, and he said: Helam, I baptize thee, having authority from the Almighty God, as a testimony that ye have entered into a covenant to serve him until you are dead as to the mortal body; and may the Spirit of the Lord be poured out upon you; and may he grant unto you eternal life, through the redemption of Christ, whom he has prepared from the foundation of the world.

14 And after Alma had said these words, both Alma and Helam were buried in the water; and they arose and came forth out of the water rejoicing, being filled with the Spirit.

15 And again, Alma took another, and went forth a second time into the water, and baptized him according to the first, only he did not bury himself again in the water.

16 And after this manner he did baptize every one that went forth to the place of Mormon; and they were in number about two hundred and four souls; yea, and they were baptized in the waters of Mormon, and were filled with the grace of God.

17 And they were called the church of God, or the church of Christ, from that time forward. And it came to pass that whosoever was baptized by the power and authority of God was added to his church.

18 And it came to pass that Alma, having authority from God, ordained priests; even one priest to every fifty of their number did he ordain to preach unto them, and to teach them concerning the things pertaining to the kingdom of God.

19 And he commanded them that they should teach nothing save it were the things which he had taught, and which had been spoken by the mouth of the holy prophets.

20 Yea, even he commanded them that they should preach nothing save it were repentance and faith on the Lord, who had redeemed his people.

21 And he commanded them that there should be no contention one with another, but that they should look forward with one eye, having one faith and one baptism, having their hearts knit together in unity and in love one towards another.

22 And thus he commanded them to preach. And thus they became the children of God.

23 And he commanded them that they should observe the sabbath day, and keep it holy, and also every day they should give thanks to the Lord their God.

Date _____
☐ Completed

Date _____
☐ Completed

24 And he also commanded them that the priests whom he had ordained should labor with their own hands for their support.

25 And there was one day in every week that was set apart that they should gather themselves together to teach the people, and to worship the Lord their God, and also, as often as it was in their power, to assemble themselves together.

26 And the priests were not to depend upon the people for their support; but for their labor they were to receive the grace of God, that they might wax strong in the Spirit, having the knowledge of God, that they might teach with power and authority from God.

27 And again Alma commanded that the people of the church should impart of their substance, every one according to that which he had; if he have more abundantly he should impart more abundantly; and of him that had but little, but little should be required; and to him that had not should be given.

28 And thus they should impart of their substance of their own free will and good desires towards God, and to those priests that stood in need, yea, and to every needy, naked soul.

29 And this he said unto them, having been commanded of God; and they did walk uprightly before God, imparting to one another both temporally and spiritually according to their needs and their wants.

30 And now it came to pass that all this was done in Mormon, yea, by the waters of Mormon, in the forest that was near the waters of Mormon; yea, the place of Mormon, the waters of Mormon, the forest of Mormon, how beautiful are they to the eyes of them who there came to the knowledge of their Redeemer; yea, and how blessed are they, for they shall sing to his praise forever.

31 And these things were done in the borders of the land, that they might not come to the knowledge of the king.

32 But behold, it came to pass that the king, having discovered a movement among the people, sent his servants to watch them. Therefore on the day that they were assembling themselves together to hear the word of the Lord they were discovered unto the king.

33 And now the king said that Alma was stirring up the people to rebellion against him; therefore he sent his army to destroy them.

34 And it came to pass that Alma and the people of the Lord were apprised of the coming of the king's army; therefore they took their tents and their families and departed into the wilderness.

35 And they were in number about four hundred and fifty souls.

Date _____
☐ Completed

Date _____
☐ Completed

Mosiah 19

1 And it came to pass that the army of the king returned, having searched in vain for the people of the Lord.

2 And now behold, the forces of the king were small, having been reduced, and there began to be a division among the remainder of the people.

3 And the lesser part began to breathe out threatenings against the king, and there began to be a great contention among them.

4 And now there was a man among them whose name was Gideon, and he being a strong man and an enemy to the king, therefore he drew his sword, and swore in his wrath that he would slay the king.

5 And it came to pass that he fought with the king; and when the king saw that he was about to overpower him, he fled and ran and got upon the tower which was near the temple.

6 And Gideon pursued after him and was about to get upon the tower to slay the king, and the king cast his eyes round about towards the land of Shemlon, and behold, the army of the Lamanites were within the borders of the land.

7 And now the king cried out in the anguish of his soul, saying: Gideon, spare me, for the Lamanites are upon us, and they will destroy us; yea, they will destroy my people.

8 And now the king was not so much concerned about his people as he was about his own life; nevertheless, Gideon did spare his life.

Date _____
☐ Completed

9 And the king commanded the people that they should flee before the Lamanites, and he himself did go before them, and they did flee into the wilderness, with their women and their children.

10 And it came to pass that the Lamanites did pursue them, and did overtake them, and began to slay them.

11 Now it came to pass that the king commanded them that all the men should leave their wives and their children, and flee before the Lamanites.

12 Now there were many that would not leave them, but had rather stay and perish with them. And the rest left their wives and their children and fled.

13 And it came to pass that those who tarried with their wives and their children caused that their fair daughters should stand forth and plead with the Lamanites that they would not slay them.

14 And it came to pass that the Lamanites had compassion on them, for they were charmed with the beauty of their women.

Date _____
☐ Completed

15 Therefore the Lamanites did spare their lives, and took them captives and carried them back to the land of Nephi, and granted unto them that they might possess the land, under the conditions that they would deliver up king Noah into the hands of the Lamanites, and deliver up their

165

property, even one half of all they possessed, one half of their gold, and their silver, and all their precious things, and thus they should pay tribute to the king of the Lamanites from year to year.

16 And now there was one of the sons of the king among those that were taken captive, whose name was Limhi.

17 And now Limhi was desirous that his father should not be destroyed; nevertheless, Limhi was not ignorant of the iniquities of his father, he himself being a just man.

18 And it came to pass that Gideon sent men into the wilderness secretly, to search for the king and those that were with him. And it came to pass that they met the people in the wilderness, all save the king and his priests.

19 Now they had sworn in their hearts that they would return to the land of Nephi, and if their wives and their children were slain, and also those that had tarried with them, that they would seek revenge, and also perish with them.

20 And the king commanded them that they should not return; and they were angry with the king, and caused that he should suffer, even unto death by fire.

21 And they were about to take the priests also and put them to death, and they fled before them.

22 And it came to pass that they were about to return to the land of Nephi, and they met the men of Gideon. And the men of Gideon told them of all that had happened to their wives and their children; and that the Lamanites had granted unto them that they might possess the land by paying a tribute to the Lamanites of one half of all they possessed.

23 And the people told the men of Gideon that they had slain the king, and his priests had fled from them farther into the wilderness.

24 And it came to pass that after they had ended the ceremony, that they returned to the land of Nephi, rejoicing, because their wives and their children were not slain; and they told Gideon what they had done to the king.

25 And it came to pass that the king of the Lamanites made an oath unto them, that his people should not slay them.

26 And also Limhi, being the son of the king, having the kingdom conferred upon him by the people, made oath unto the king of the Lamanites that his people should pay tribute unto him, even one half of all they possessed.

27 And it came to pass that Limhi began to establish the kingdom and to establish peace among his people.

28 And the king of the Lamanites set guards round about the land, that he might keep the people of Limhi in the land, that they might not depart into the wilderness; and he did support his guards out of the tribute which he did receive from the Nephites.

29 And now king Limhi did have continual peace in his kingdom for the space of two years, that the Lamanites did not molest them nor seek to destroy them.

Date _____
☐ Completed

Date _____
☐ Completed

Mosiah 20

1 Now there was a place in Shemlon where the daughters of the Lamanites did gather themselves together to sing, and to dance, and to make themselves merry.

2 And it came to pass that there was one day a small number of them gathered together to sing and to dance.

3 And now the priests of king Noah, being ashamed to return to the city of Nephi, yea, and also fearing that the people would slay them, therefore they durst not return to their wives and their children.

4 And having tarried in the wilderness, and having discovered the daughters of the Lamanites, they laid and watched them;

5 And when there were but few of them gathered together to dance, they came forth out of their secret places and took them and carried them into the wilderness; yea, twenty and four of the daughters of the Lamanites they carried into the wilderness.

6 And it came to pass that when the Lamanites found that their daughters had been missing, they were angry with the people of Limhi, for they thought it was the people of Limhi.

Date _____
☐ Completed

7 Therefore they sent their armies forth; yea, even the king himself went before his people; and they went up to the land of Nephi to destroy the people of Limhi.

8 And now Limhi had discovered them from the tower, even all their preparations for war did he discover; therefore he gathered his people together, and laid wait for them in the fields and in the forests.

9 And it came to pass that when the Lamanites had come up, that the people of Limhi began to fall upon them from their waiting places, and began to slay them.

10 And it came to pass that the battle became exceedingly sore, for they fought like lions for their prey.

11 And it came to pass that the people of Limhi began to drive the Lamanites before them; yet they were not half so numerous as the Lamanites. But they fought for their lives, and for their wives, and for their children; therefore they exerted themselves and like dragons did they fight.

12 And it came to pass that they found the king of the Lamanites among the number of their dead; yet he was not dead, having been wounded and left upon the ground, so speedy was the flight of his people.

Date _____
☐ Completed

13 And they took him and bound up his wounds, and brought him before Limhi, and said: Behold, here is the king of the Lamanites; he having received a wound has fallen among their dead, and they have left him; and behold, we have brought him before you; and now let us slay him.

14 But Limhi said unto them: Ye shall not slay him, but bring him hither that I may see him. And they brought him. And Limhi said unto him: What cause have ye to come up to war against my people? Behold, my people have not broken the oath that I made unto you; therefore, why should ye break the oath which ye made unto my people?

15 And now the king said: I have broken the oath because thy people did carry away the daughters of my people; therefore, in my anger I did cause my people to come up to war against thy people.

16 And now Limhi had heard nothing concerning this matter; therefore he said: I will search among my people and whosoever has done this thing shall perish. Therefore he caused a search to be made among his people.

17 Now when Gideon had heard these things, he being the king's captain, he went forth and said unto the king: I pray thee forbear, and do not search this people, and lay not this thing to their charge.

18 For do ye not remember the priests of thy father, whom this people sought to destroy? And are they not in the wilderness? And are not they the ones who have stolen the daughters of the Lamanites?

19 And now, behold, and tell the king of these things, that he may tell his people that they may be pacified towards us; for behold they are already preparing to come against us; and behold also there are but few of us.

20 And behold, they come with their numerous hosts; and except the king doth pacify them towards us we must perish.

21 For are not the words of Abinadi fulfilled, which he prophesied against us—and all this because we would not hearken unto the words of the Lord, and turn from our iniquities?

22 And now let us pacify the king, and we fulfil the oath which we have made unto him; for it is better that we should be in bondage than that we should lose our lives; therefore, let us put a stop to the shedding of so much blood.

23 And now Limhi told the king all the things concerning his father, and the priests that had fled into the wilderness, and attributed the carrying away of their daughters to them.

24 And it came to pass that the king was pacified towards his people; and he said unto them: Let us go forth to meet my people, without arms; and I swear unto you with an oath that my people shall not slay thy people.

25 And it came to pass that they followed the king, and went forth without arms to meet the Lamanites. And it came to pass that they did meet the Lamanites; and the king of the Lamanites did bow himself down before them, and did plead in behalf of the people of Limhi.

26 And when the Lamanites saw the people of Limhi, that they were without arms, they had compassion on them and were pacified towards them, and returned with their king in peace to their own land.

Date _____
☐ Completed

Date _____
☐ Completed

Mosiah 21

1 And it came to pass that Limhi and his people returned to the city of Nephi, and began to dwell in the land again in peace.

2 And it came to pass that after many days the Lamanites began again to be stirred up in anger against the Nephites, and they began to come into the borders of the land round about.

3 Now they durst not slay them, because of the oath which their king had made unto Limhi; but they would smite them on their cheeks, and exercise authority over them; and began to put heavy burdens upon their backs, and drive them as they would a dumb ass—

4 Yea, all this was done that the word of the Lord might be fulfilled.

5 And now the afflictions of the Nephites were great, and there was no way that they could deliver themselves out of their hands, for the Lamanites had surrounded them on every side.

6 And it came to pass that the people began to murmur with the king because of their afflictions; and they began to be desirous to go against them to battle. And they did afflict the king sorely with their complaints; therefore he granted unto them that they should do according to their desires.

7 And they gathered themselves together again, and put on their armor, and went forth against the Lamanites to drive them out of their land.

8 And it came to pass that the Lamanites did beat them, and drove them back, and slew many of them.

9 And now there was a great mourning and lamentation among the people of Limhi, the widow mourning for her husband, the son and the daughter mourning for their father, and the brothers for their brethren.

10 Now there were a great many widows in the land, and they did cry mightily from day to day, for a great fear of the Lamanites had come upon them.

11 And it came to pass that their continual cries did stir up the remainder of the people of Limhi to anger against the Lamanites; and they went again to battle, but they were driven back again, suffering much loss.

12 Yea, they went again even the third time, and suffered in the like manner; and those that were not slain returned again to the city of Nephi.

13 And they did humble themselves even to the dust, subjecting themselves to the yoke of bondage, submitting themselves to be smitten, and to be driven to and fro, and burdened, according to the desires of their enemies.

14 And they did humble themselves even in the depths of humility; and they did cry mightily to God; yea, even all the day long did they cry unto their God that he would deliver them out of their afflictions.

15 And now the Lord was slow to hear their cry because of their iniquities;

nevertheless the Lord did hear their cries, and began to soften the hearts of the Lamanites that they began to ease their burdens; yet the Lord did not see fit to deliver them out of bondage.

16 And it came to pass that they began to prosper by degrees in the land, and began to raise grain more abundantly, and flocks, and herds, that they did not suffer with hunger.

17 Now there was a great number of women, more than there was of men; therefore king Limhi commanded that every man should impart to the support of the widows and their children, that they might not perish with hunger; and this they did because of the greatness of their number that had been slain.

18 Now the people of Limhi kept together in a body as much as it was possible, and secured their grain and their flocks;

19 And the king himself did not trust his person without the walls of the city, unless he took his guards with him, fearing that he might by some means fall into the hands of the Lamanites.

20 And he caused that his people should watch the land round about, that by some means they might take those priests that fled into the wilderness, who had stolen the daughters of the Lamanites, and that had caused such a great destruction to come upon them.

21 For they were desirous to take them that they might punish them; for they had come into the land of Nephi by night, and carried off their grain and many of their precious things; therefore they laid wait for them.

22 And it came to pass that there was no more disturbance between the Lamanites and the people of Limhi, even until the time that Ammon and his brethren came into the land.

23 And the king having been without the gates of the city with his guard, discovered Ammon and his brethren; and supposing them to be priests of Noah therefore he caused that they should be taken, and bound, and cast into prison. And had they been the priests of Noah he would have caused that they should be put to death.

24 But when he found that they were not, but that they were his brethren, and had come from the land of Zarahemla, he was filled with exceedingly great joy.

25 Now king Limhi had sent, previous to the coming of Ammon, a small number of men to search for the land of Zarahemla; but they could not find it, and they were lost in the wilderness.

26 Nevertheless, they did find a land which had been peopled; yea, a land which was covered with dry bones; yea, a land which had been peopled and which had been destroyed; and they, having supposed it to be the land of Zarahemla, returned to the land of Nephi, having arrived in the borders of the land not many days before the coming of Ammon.

Date _____
☐ Completed

Date _____
☐ Completed

27 And they brought a record with them, even a record of the people whose bones they had found; and it was engraven on plates of ore.

28 And now Limhi was again filled with joy on learning from the mouth of Ammon that king Mosiah had a gift from God, whereby he could interpret such engravings; yea, and Ammon also did rejoice.

29 Yet Ammon and his brethren were filled with sorrow because so many of their brethren had been slain;

30 And also that king Noah and his priests had caused the people to commit so many sins and iniquities against God; and they also did mourn for the death of Abinadi; and also for the departure of Alma and the people that went with him, who had formed a church of God through the strength and power of God, and faith on the words which had been spoken by Abinadi.

31 Yea, they did mourn for their departure, for they knew not whither they had fled. Now they would have gladly joined with them, for they themselves had entered into a covenant with God to serve him and keep his commandments.

32 And now since the coming of Ammon, king Limhi had also entered into a covenant with God, and also many of his people, to serve him and keep his commandments.

33 And it came to pass that king Limhi and many of his people were desirous to be baptized; but there was none in the land that had authority from God. And Ammon declined doing this thing, considering himself an unworthy servant.

34 Therefore they did not at that time form themselves into a church, waiting upon the Spirit of the Lord. Now they were desirous to become even as Alma and his brethren, who had fled into the wilderness.

35 They were desirous to be baptized as a witness and a testimony that they were willing to serve God with all their hearts; nevertheless they did prolong the time; and an account of their baptism shall be given hereafter.

36 And now all the study of Ammon and his people, and king Limhi and his people, was to deliver themselves out of the hands of the Lamanites and from bondage.

Notes

Date _____
☐ Completed

Date _____
☐ Completed

175

Mosiah

Chapter 22—Review

Sight (Memorization) Words

father	been	both	half	swear	fro

Phonics Application

- *Complex Consonants:* blends that include three consonants, two consonants that sounds like a single letter, and consonant and vowel clusters. The complex consonants are QU, TCH, CK, GN, MB, KN, WR.
  - *Silent Consonant:*
    - GN—the G is silent (example: **gn**at)
    - MB—the B is silent (example: co**mb**)
    - KN—the K is silent (example: **kn**ot)
    - WR—the W is silent (example: **wr**ap)
  - *Sound alike final consonant sounds:*
    - GE and DGE; these blends make the same sound (example: a**ge** and e**dge).**
    - K, CK, and KE; these blends make the same sound (example: lin**k**, ba**ck**, ba**ke).**
  - *Soft Consonants:*
    - *G*—when G is followed by E, I, and Y it makes the J sound /j/ (example: **ge**m, **gi**st, **gy**m).
    - *C*—when C is followed by E, I , and Y, it makes the S sound /s/ (example: ri**ce**, **ci**ty, **cy**st).
- *Rule:*
  - *C* comes before A, E, and U (can, cop, cup)
  - *K* comes before I and E (kit, key)

Recommended (Age Appropriate) Reading Chunks

- Versus 1–5
- Versus 6–11
- Versus 12–16

Gospel Principle Review/Activity

- How did the Lord help the people of Limhi escape?
- How did Ammon help? How did Gideon help?
- *Activity:* The Lamanites followed the people of Limhi's tracks to try and hunt them down. Tracks are usually footprints showing where a person or an animal has gone. What type of tracks can you find in your neighborhood? When you find a track, see if you can figure out what animal or object it belongs to. (You might want to check out a library book or encyclopedia to help you know what types of tracks you are looking at.)

Word Patterns—Review

Parents read the clue and children fill in the blank words in the word box.

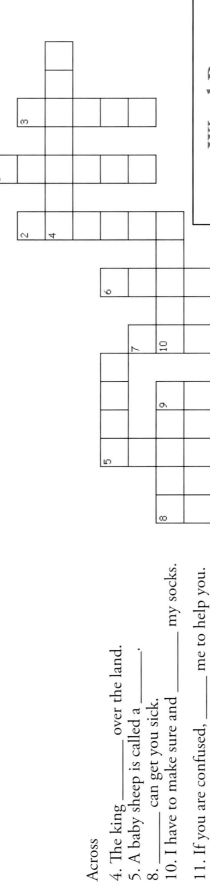

Word Box

match	lamb
bridge	city
smoke	gym
branch	snack
reigned	ask
kneel	germs
large	

Across

4. The king _____ over the land.
5. A baby sheep is called a _____.
8. _____ can get you sick.
10. I have to make sure and _____ my socks.
11. If you are confused, _____ me to help you.

Down

1. We had to go one at a time as we crossed the _____.
2. The tree had only one _____.
3. When we pray we often _____.
4. The opposite of small is _____.
5. Los Angeles is a big _____.
6. The campfire gave off a lot of _____.
7. We go to the _____ for P.E.
8. When I am hungry I eat a _____.

Mosiah 22

1 And now it came to pass that Ammon and king Limhi began to consult with the people how they should deliver themselves out of bondage; and even they did cause that all the people should gather themselves together; and this they did that they might have the voice of the people concerning the matter.

2 And it came to pass that they could find no way to deliver themselves out of bondage, except it were to take their women and children, and their flocks, and their herds, and their tents, and depart into the wilderness; for the Lamanites being so numerous, it was impossible for the people of Limhi to contend with them, thinking to deliver themselves out of bondage by the sword.

3 Now it came to pass that Gideon went forth and stood before the king, and said unto him: Now O king, thou hast hitherto hearkened unto my words many times when we have been contending with our brethren, the Lamanites.

4 And now O king, if thou hast not found me to be an unprofitable servant, or if thou hast hitherto listened to my words in any degree, and they have been of service to thee, even so I desire that thou wouldst listen to my words at this time, and I will be thy servant and deliver this people out of bondage.

5 And the king granted unto him that he might speak. And Gideon said unto him:

6 Behold the back pass, through the back wall, on the back side of the city. The Lamanites, or the guards of the Lamanites, by night are drunken; therefore let us send a proclamation among all this people that they gather together their flocks and herds, that they may drive them into the wilderness by night.

7 And I will go according to thy command and pay the last tribute of wine to the Lamanites, and they will be drunken; and we will pass through the secret pass on the left of their camp when they are drunken and asleep.

8 Thus we will depart with our women and our children, our flocks, and our herds into the wilderness; and we will travel around the land of Shilom.

9 And it came to pass that the king hearkened unto the words of Gideon.

10 And king Limhi caused that his people should gather their flocks together; and he sent the tribute of wine to the Lamanites; and he also sent more wine, as a present unto them; and they did drink freely of the wine which king Limhi did send unto them.

11 And it came to pass that the people of king Limhi did depart by night into the wilderness with their flocks and their herds, and they went round about the land of Shilom in the wilderness, and bent their course towards the land of Zarahemla, being led by Ammon and his brethren.

12 And they had taken all their gold, and silver, and their precious things, which they could carry, and also their provisions with them, into the wilderness; and they pursued their journey.

13 And after being many days in the wilderness they arrived in the land of Zarahemla, and joined Mosiah's people, and became his subjects.

14 And it came to pass that Mosiah received them with joy; and he also received their records, and also the records which had been found by the people of Limhi.

15 And now it came to pass when the Lamanites had found that the people of Limhi had departed out of the land by night, that they sent an army into the wilderness to pursue them;

16 And after they had pursued them two days, they could no longer follow their tracks; therefore they were lost in the wilderness.

Date _____

☐ Completed

Mosiah

Chapter 23

Sight (Memorization) Words

love

Word Pattern or Rule

Pattern or Rule	-ei
Pattern words in scriptures	**eight, their, neighbor**
Location in chapter	Verses 1, 3, 5–6, 16–18, 21, 23–24, 26–29, 33–34, 36–37
Exceptions to the rule	(none listed)
Other words made from this patterns not found in chapter	reign, rein, veil, vein, weigh

Phonics Application

- *Complex Long Vowel Sounds:* long vowels make the sound of their name, but these complex long vowels do not contain the letter of the sound they are making. For example, "vein" makes the long A sound, but the vowels that combine to make the long A sound are "ei."
  - Long A—*ei*
- *Rule:* GH is silent

Recommended (Age Appropriate) Reading Chunks

- Verses 1–8
- Verses 9–15
- Verses 16–24
- Verses 25–31
- Verses 32–39

Gospel Principle Review/Activity

- Why did Alma refuse to be king? What is it like to live under a king?
- Who did the Lamanites find?
- *Activity:* Alma taught the people to "trust no one to be your teacher nor your minister, except he be a man of God." Learning who and how to trust is difficult. To learn the value of trust, play a game called "fall back."
  1) Have a person stand behind you.
  2) Stand directly in front of that person with your back to him.
  3) Lock your knees and fall backward.
  4) The goal of the person behind you is to catch you.
  5) Your goal is to trust and not doubt that the person will catch you.

Word Patterns

ei _____

Words made with –ei word pattern.
Use alphabet letters to create words.

Mosiah 23

1 Now Alma, having been warned of the Lord that the armies of king Noah would come upon them, and having made it known to his people, therefore they gathered together their flocks, and took of their grain, and departed into the wilderness before the armies of king Noah.

2 And the Lord did strengthen them, that the people of king Noah could not overtake them to destroy them.

3 And they fled eight days' journey into the wilderness.

4 And they came to a land, yea, even a very beautiful and pleasant land, a land of pure water.

5 And they pitched their tents, and began to till the ground, and began to build buildings; yea, they were industrious, and did labor exceedingly.

6 And the people were desirous that Alma should be their king, for he was beloved by his people.

7 But he said unto them: Behold, it is not expedient that we should have a king; for thus saith the Lord: Ye shall not esteem one flesh above another, or one man shall not think himself above another; therefore I say unto you it is not expedient that ye should have a king.

8 Nevertheless, if it were possible that ye could always have just men to be your kings it would be well for you to have a king.

Date _____

☐ Completed

9 But remember the iniquity of king Noah and his priests; and I myself was caught in a snare, and did many things which were abominable in the sight of the Lord, which caused me sore repentance;

10 Nevertheless, after much tribulation, the Lord did hear my cries, and did answer my prayers, and has made me an instrument in his hands in bringing so many of you to a knowledge of his truth.

11 Nevertheless, in this I do not glory, for I am unworthy to glory of myself.

12 And now I say unto you, ye have been oppressed by king Noah, and have been in bondage to him and his priests, and have been brought into iniquity by them; therefore ye were bound with the bands of iniquity.

13 And now as ye have been delivered by the power of God out of these bonds; yea, even out of the hands of king Noah and his people, and also from the bonds of iniquity, even so I desire that ye should stand fast in this liberty wherewith ye have been made free, and that ye trust no man to be a king over you.

14 And also trust no one to be your teacher nor your minister, except he be a man of God, walking in his ways and keeping his commandments.

15 Thus did Alma teach his people, that every man should love his neighbor as himself, that there should be no contention among them.

Date _____

☐ Completed

16 And now, Alma was their high priest, he being the founder of their church.

17 And it came to pass that none received authority to preach or to teach except it were by him from God. Therefore he consecrated all their priests and all their teachers; and none were consecrated except they were just men.

18 Therefore they did watch over their people, and did nourish them with things pertaining to righteousness.

19 And it came to pass that they began to prosper exceedingly in the land; and they called the land Helam.

20 And it came to pass that they did multiply and prosper exceedingly in the land of Helam; and they built a city, which they called the city of Helam.

21 Nevertheless the Lord seeth fit to chasten his people; yea, he trieth their patience and their faith.

22 Nevertheless—whosoever putteth his trust in him the same shall be lifted up at the last day. Yea, and thus it was with this people.

23 For behold, I will show unto you that they were brought into bondage, and none could deliver them but the Lord their God, yea, even the God of Abraham and Isaac and of Jacob.

24 And it came to pass that he did deliver them, and he did show forth his mighty power unto them, and great were their rejoicings.

25 For behold, it came to pass that while they were in the land of Helam, yea, in the city of Helam, while tilling the land round about, behold an army of the Lamanites was in the borders of the land.

26 Now it came to pass that the brethren of Alma fled from their fields, and gathered themselves together in the city of Helam; and they were much frightened because of the appearance of the Lamanites.

27 But Alma went forth and stood among them, and exhorted them that they should not be frightened, but that they should remember the Lord their God and he would deliver them.

28 Therefore they hushed their fears, and began to cry unto the Lord that he would soften the hearts of the Lamanites, that they would spare them, and their wives, and their children.

29 And it came to pass that the Lord did soften the hearts of the Lamanites. And Alma and his brethren went forth and delivered themselves up into their hands; and the Lamanites took possession of the land of Helam.

30 Now the armies of the Lamanites, which had followed after the people of king Limhi, had been lost in the wilderness for many days.

31 And behold, they had found those priests of king Noah, in a place which they called Amulon; and they had begun to possess the land of Amulon and had begun to till the ground.

Date _____
☐ Completed

Date _____
☐ Completed

32 Now the name of the leader of those priests was Amulon.

33 And it came to pass that Amulon did plead with the Lamanites; and he also sent forth their wives, who were the daughters of the Lamanites, to plead with their brethren, that they should not destroy their husbands.

34 And the Lamanites had compassion on Amulon and his brethren, and did not destroy them, because of their wives.

35 And Amulon and his brethren did join the Lamanites, and they were traveling in the wilderness in search of the land of Nephi when they discovered the land of Helam, which was possessed by Alma and his brethren.

36 And it came to pass that the Lamanites promised unto Alma and his brethren, that if they would show them the way which led to the land of Nephi that they would grant unto them their lives and their liberty.

37 But after Alma had shown them the way that led to the land of Nephi the Lamanites would not keep their promise; but they set guards round about the land of Helam, over Alma and his brethren.

38 And the remainder of them went to the land of Nephi; and a part of them returned to the land of Helam, and also brought with them the wives and the children of the guards who had been left in the land.

39 And the king of the Lamanites had granted unto Amulon that he should be a king and a ruler over his people, who were in the land of Helam; nevertheless he should have no power to do anything contrary to the will of the king of the Lamanites.

Date _____

☐ Completed

Mosiah 24

1 And it came to pass that Amulon did gain favor in the eyes of the king of the Lamanites; therefore, the king of the Lamanites granted unto him and his brethren that they should be appointed teachers over his people, yea, even over the people who were in the land of Shemlon, and in the land of Shilom, and in the land of Amulon.

2 For the Lamanites had taken possession of all these lands; therefore, the king of the Lamanites had appointed kings over all these lands.

3 And now the name of the king of the Lamanites was Laman, being called after the name of his father; and therefore he was called king Laman. And he was king over a numerous people.

4 And he appointed teachers of the brethren of Amulon in every land which was possessed by his people; and thus the language of Nephi began to be taught among all the people of the Lamanites.

5 And they were a people friendly one with another; nevertheless they knew not God; neither did the brethren of Amulon teach them anything concerning the Lord their God, neither the law of Moses; nor did they teach them the words of Abinadi;

6 But they taught them that they should keep their record, and that they might write one to another.

Date _____
☐ Completed

7 And thus the Lamanites began to increase in riches, and began to trade one with another and wax great, and began to be a cunning and a wise people, as to the wisdom of the world, yea, a very cunning people, delighting in all manner of wickedness and plunder, except it were among their own brethren.

8 And now it came to pass that Amulon began to exercise authority over Alma and his brethren, and began to persecute him, and cause that his children should persecute their children.

9 For Amulon knew Alma, that he had been one of the king's priests, and that it was he that believed the words of Abinadi and was driven out before the king, and therefore he was wroth with him; for he was subject to king Laman, yet he exercised authority over them, and put tasks upon them, and put task-masters over them.

10 And it came to pass that so great were their afflictions that they began to cry mightily to God.

11 And Amulon commanded them that they should stop their cries; and he put guards over them to watch them, that whosoever should be found calling upon God should be put to death.

Date _____
☐ Completed

12 And Alma and his people did not raise their voices to the Lord their God, but did pour out their hearts to him; and he did know the thoughts of their hearts.

13 And it came to pass that the voice of the Lord came to them in their afflictions, saying: Lift up your heads and be of good comfort, for I know of the covenant which ye have made unto me; and I will covenant with my people and deliver them out of bondage.

14 And I will also ease the burdens which are put upon your shoulders, that even you cannot feel them upon your backs, even while you are in bondage; and this will I do that ye may stand as witnesses for me hereafter, and that ye may know of a surety that I, the Lord God, do visit my people in their afflictions.

15 And now it came to pass that the burdens which were laid upon Alma and his brethren were made light; yea, the Lord did strengthen them that they could bear up their burdens with ease, and they did submit cheerfully and with patience to all the will of the Lord.

16 And it came to pass that so great was their faith and their patience that the voice of the Lord came unto them again, saying: Be of good comfort, for on the morrow I will deliver you out of bondage.

17 And he said unto Alma: Thou shalt go before this people, and I will go with thee and deliver this people out of bondage.

18 Now it came to pass that Alma and his people in the night-time gathered their flocks together, and also of their grain; yea, even all the night-time were they gathering the flocks together.

19 And in the morning the Lord caused a deep sleep to come upon the Lamanites, yea, and all their task-masters were in a profound sleep.

20 And Alma and his people departed into the wilderness; and when they had traveled all day they pitched their tents in a valley, and they called the valley Alma, because he led their way in the wilderness.

21 Yea, and in the valley of Alma they poured out their thanks to God because he had been merciful unto them, and eased their burdens, and had delivered them out of bondage; for they were in bondage, and none could deliver them except it were the Lord their God.

22 And they gave thanks to God, yea, all their men and all their women and all their children that could speak lifted their voices in the praises of their God.

23 And now the Lord said unto Alma: Haste thee and get thou and this people out of this land, for the Lamanites have awakened and do pursue thee; therefore get thee out of this land, and I will stop the Lamanites in this valley that they come no further in pursuit of this people.

24 And it came to pass that they departed out of the valley, and took their journey into the wilderness.

25 And after they had been in the wilderness twelve days they arrived in the land of Zarahemla; and king Mosiah did also receive them with joy.

Date _____
☐ Completed

Date _____
☐ Completed

Mosiah 25

1 And now king Mosiah caused that all the people should be gathered together.

2 Now there were not so many of the children of Nephi, or so many of those who were descendants of Nephi, as there were of the people of Zarahemla, who was a descendant of Mulek, and those who came with him into the wilderness.

3 And there were not so many of the people of Nephi and of the people of Zarahemla as there were of the Lamanites; yea, they were not half so numerous.

4 And now all the people of Nephi were assembled together, and also all the people of Zarahemla, and they were gathered together in two bodies.

5 And it came to pass that Mosiah did read, and caused to be read, the records of Zeniff to his people; yea, he read the records of the people of Zeniff, from the time they left the land of Zarahemla until they returned again.

6 And he also read the account of Alma and his brethren, and all their afflictions, from the time they left the land of Zarahemla until the time they returned again.

7 And now, when Mosiah had made an end of reading the records, his people who tarried in the land were struck with wonder and amazement.

8 For they knew not what to think; for when they beheld those that had been delivered out of bondage they were filled with exceedingly great joy.

9 And again, when they thought of their brethren who had been slain by the Lamanites they were filled with sorrow, and even shed many tears of sorrow.

10 And again, when they thought of the immediate goodness of God, and his power in delivering Alma and his brethren out of the hands of the Lamanites and of bondage, they did raise their voices and give thanks to God.

11 And again, when they thought upon the Lamanites, who were their brethren, of their sinful and polluted state, they were filled with pain and anguish for the welfare of their souls.

12 And it came to pass that those who were the children of Amulon and his brethren, who had taken to wife the daughters of the Lamanites, were displeased with the conduct of their fathers, and they would no longer be called by the names of their fathers, therefore they took upon themselves the name of Nephi, that they might be called the children of Nephi and be numbered among those who were called Nephites.

13 And now all the people of Zarahemla were numbered with the Nephites, and this because the kingdom had been conferred upon none but those who were descendants of Nephi.

14 And now it came to pass that when Mosiah had made an end of speaking and reading to the people, he desired that Alma should also speak to the people.

15 And Alma did speak unto them, when they were assembled together in large bodies, and he went from one body to another, preaching unto the people repentance and faith on the Lord.

16 And he did exhort the people of Limhi and his brethren, all those that had been delivered out of bondage, that they should remember that it was the Lord that did deliver them.

17 And it came to pass that after Alma had taught the people many things, and had made an end of speaking to them, that king Limhi was desirous that he might be baptized; and all his people were desirous that they might be baptized also.

18 Therefore, Alma did go forth into the water and did baptize them; yea, he did baptize them after the manner he did his brethren in the waters of Mormon; yea, and as many as he did baptize did belong to the church of God; and this because of their belief on the words of Alma.

19 And it came to pass that king Mosiah granted unto Alma that he might establish churches throughout all the land of Zarahemla; and gave him power to ordain priests and teachers over every church.

20 Now this was done because there were so many people that they could not all be governed by one teacher; neither could they all hear the word of God in one assembly;

21 Therefore they did assemble themselves together in different bodies, being called churches; every church having their priests and their teachers, and every priest preaching the word according as it was delivered to him by the mouth of Alma.

22 And thus, notwithstanding there being many churches they were all one church, yea, even the church of God; for there was nothing preached in all the churches except it were repentance and faith in God.

23 And now there were seven churches in the land of Zarahemla. And it came to pass that whosoever were desirous to take upon them the name of Christ, or of God, they did join the churches of God;

24 And they were called the people of God. And the Lord did pour out his Spirit upon them, and they were blessed, and prospered in the land.

Date _____

☐ Completed

Date _____

☐ Completed

Mosiah 26

1 Now it came to pass that there were many of the rising generation that could not understand the words of king Benjamin, being little children at the time he spake unto his people; and they did not believe the tradition of their fathers.

2 They did not believe what had been said concerning the resurrection of the dead, neither did they believe concerning the coming of Christ.

3 And now because of their unbelief they could not understand the word of God; and their hearts were hardened.

4 And they would not be baptized; neither would they join the church. And they were a separate people as to their faith, and remained so ever after, even in their carnal and sinful state; for they would not call upon the Lord their God.

5 And now in the reign of Mosiah they were not half so numerous as the people of God; but because of the dissensions among the brethren they became more numerous.

6 For it came to pass that they did deceive many with their flattering words, who were in the church, and did cause them to commit many sins; therefore it became expedient that those who committed sin, that were in the church, should be admonished by the church.

7 And it came to pass that they were brought before the priests, and delivered up unto the priests by the teachers; and the priests brought them before Alma, who was the high priest.

Date _____
☐ Completed

8 Now king Mosiah had given Alma the authority over the church.

9 And it came to pass that Alma did not know concerning them; but there were many witnesses against them; yea, the people stood and testified of their iniquity in abundance.

10 Now there had not any such thing happened before in the church; therefore Alma was troubled in his spirit, and he caused that they should be brought before the king.

11 And he said unto the king: Behold, here are many whom we have brought before thee, who are accused of their brethren; yea, and they have been taken in divers iniquities. And they do not repent of their iniquities; therefore we have brought them before thee, that thou mayest judge them according to their crimes.

12 But king Mosiah said unto Alma: Behold, I judge them not; therefore I deliver them into people hands to be judged.

13 And now the spirit of Alma was again troubled; and he went and inquired of the Lord what he should do concerning this matter, for he feared that he should do wrong in the sight of God.

Date _____
☐ Completed

14 And it came to pass that after he had poured out his whole soul to God, the voice of the Lord came to him, saying:

15 Blessed art thou, Alma, and blessed are they who were baptized in the waters of Mormon. Thou art blessed because of people exceeding faith in the words alone of my servant Abinadi.

16 And blessed are they because of their exceeding faith in the words alone which thou hast spoken unto them.

17 And blessed art thou because thou hast established a church among this people; and they shall be established, and they shall be my people.

18 Yea, blessed is this people who are willing to bear my name; for in my name shall they be called; and they are mine.

19 And because thou hast inquired of me concerning the transgressor, thou art blessed.

20 Thou art my servant; and I covenant with thee that thou shalt have eternal life; and thou shalt serve me and go forth in my name, and shalt gather together my sheep.

21 And he that will hear my voice shall be my sheep; and him shall ye receive into the church, and him will I also receive.

22 For behold, this is my church; whosoever is baptized shall be baptized unto repentance. And whomsoever ye receive shall believe in my name; and him will I freely forgive.

23 For it is I that taketh upon me the sins of the world; for it is I that hath created them; and it is I that granteth unto him that believeth unto the end a place at my right hand.

24 For behold, in my name are they called; and if they know me they shall come forth, and shall have a place eternally at my right hand.

25 And it shall come to pass that when the second trump shall sound then shall they that never knew me come forth and shall stand before me.

26 And then shall they know that I am the Lord their God, that I am their Redeemer; but they would not be redeemed.

27 And then I will confess unto them that I never knew them; and they shall depart into everlasting fire prepared for the devil and his angels.

28 Therefore I say unto you, that he that will not hear my voice, the same shall ye not receive into my church, for him I will not receive at the last day.

29 Therefore I say unto you, Go; and whosoever transgresseth against me, him shall ye judge according to the sins which he has committed; and if he confess his sins before thee and me, and repenteth in the sincerity of his heart, him shall ye forgive, and I will forgive him also.

30 Yea, and as often as my people repent will I forgive them their trespasses against me.

31 And ye shall also forgive one another your trespasses; for verily I say

unto you, he that forgiveth not his neighbor's trespasses when he says that he repents, the same hath brought himself under condemnation.

32 Now I say unto you, Go; and whosoever will not repent of his sins the same shall not be numbered among my people; and this shall be observed from this time forward.

33 And it came to pass when Alma had heard these words he wrote them down that he might have them, and that he might judge the people of that church according to the commandments of God.

34 And it came to pass that Alma went and judged those that had been taken in iniquity, according to the word of the Lord.

35 And whosoever repented of their sins and did confess them, them he did number among the people of the church;

36 And those that would not confess their sins and repent of their iniquity, the same were not numbered among the people of the church, and their names were blotted out.

37 And it came to pass that Alma did regulate all the affairs of the church; and they began again to have peace and to prosper exceedingly in the affairs of the church, walking circumspectly before God, receiving many, and baptizing many.

38 And now all these things did Alma and his fellow laborers do who were over the church, walking in all diligence, teaching the word of God in all things, suffering all manner of afflictions, being persecuted by all those who did not belong to the church of God.

39 And they did admonish their brethren; and they were also admonished, every one by the word of God, according to his sins, or to the sins which he had committed, being commanded of God to pray without ceasing, and to give thanks in all things.

Date _____

☐ Completed

Mosiah

Chapter 27

Sight (Memorization) Words

began

Word Pattern or Rule

Pattern or Rule	-OW
Pattern words in scriptures	**bow, know, own**
Location in chapter	Verses 4–5, 18, 27, 31
Exceptions to the rule	bow (as in "taking a bow")
Other words made from this patterns not found in chapter	grow, show, slow, snow, blow, crow, grown, low, throw, flow, glow, sorrow, sow, tow

Phonics Application

- *Complex Long Vowel Sounds:* long vowels make the sound of their name, but these complex long vowels do not contain the letter of the sound they are making. For example, "vein" makes the long A sound, but the vowels that combine to make the long A sound are "ei."
  - Long O—*ow*

Recommended (Age Appropriate) Reading Chunks

- Verses 1–5
- Verses 6–10
- Verses 11–15
- Verses 16–21
- Verses 22–27
- Verses 28–31
- Verses 32–37

Gospel Principle Review/Activity

- Alma the Younger and the four sons of Mosiah were very disobedient. What did they do? What did their fathers do for them?
- What did the angel say to Alma? How did Alma change?
- What does it mean to "fast"?
- *Activity:* How would you feel if you were Alma the Younger and had seen an angel? Draw a picture of the scene and write down how you think Alma the Younger felt.

Word Patterns

OW

___

Words made with –ow word pattern.
Use alphabet letters to create words.

Mosiah 27

1 And now it came to pass that the persecutions which were inflicted on the church by the unbelievers became so great that the church began to murmur, and complain to their leaders concerning the matter; and they did complain to Alma. And Alma laid the case before their king, Mosiah. And Mosiah consulted with his priests.

2 And it came to pass that king Mosiah sent a proclamation throughout the land round about that there should not any unbeliever persecute any of those who belonged to the church of God.

3 And there was a strict command throughout all the churches that there should be no persecutions among them, that there should be an equality among all men;

4 That they should let no pride nor haughtiness disturb their peace; that every man should esteem his neighbor as himself, laboring with their own hands for their support.

5 Yea, and all their priests and teachers should labor with their own hands for their support, in all cases save it were in sickness, or in much want; and doing these things, they did abound in the grace of God.

6 And there began to be much peace again in the land; and the people began to be very numerous, and began to scatter abroad upon the face of the earth, yea, on the north and on the south, on the east and on the west, building large cities and villages in all quarters of the land.

7 And the Lord did visit them and prosper them, and they became a large and wealthy people.

8 Now the sons of Mosiah were numbered among the unbelievers; and also one of the sons of Alma was numbered among them, he being called Alma, after his father; nevertheless, he became a very wicked and an idolatrous man. And he was a man of many words, and did speak much flattery to the people; therefore he led many of the people to do after the manner of his iniquities.

9 And he became a great hinderment to the prosperity of the church of God; stealing away the hearts of the people; causing much dissension among the people; giving a chance for the enemy of God to exercise his power over them.

10 And now it came to pass that while he was going about to destroy the church of God, for he did go about secretly with the sons of Mosiah seeking to destroy the church, and to lead astray the people of the Lord, contrary to the commandments of God, or even the king—

11 And as I said unto you, as they were going about rebelling against God, behold, the angel of the Lord appeared unto them; and he descended as

Notes

Date _____
☐ Completed

Date _____
☐ Completed

200

it were in a cloud; and he spake as it were with a voice of thunder, which caused the earth to shake upon which they stood;

12 And so great was their astonishment, that they fell to the earth, and understood not the words which he spake unto them.

13 Nevertheless he cried again, saying: Alma, arise and stand forth, for why persecutest thou the church of God? For the Lord hath said: This is my church, and I will establish it; and nothing shall overthrow it, save it is the transgression of my people.

14 And again, the angel said: Behold, the Lord hath heard the prayers of his people, and also the prayers of his servant, Alma, who is people father; for he has prayed with much faith concerning thee that thou mightest be brought to the knowledge of the truth; therefore, for this purpose have I come to convince thee of the power and authority of God, that the prayers of his servants might be answered according to their faith.

15 And now behold, can ye dispute the power of God? For behold, doth not my voice shake the earth? And can ye not also behold me before you? And I am sent from God.

16 Now I say unto thee: Go, and remember the captivity of people fathers in the land of Helam, and in the land of Nephi; and remember how great things he has done for them; for they were in bondage, and he has delivered them. And now I say unto thee, Alma, go people way, and seek to destroy the church no more, that their prayers may be answered, and this even if thou wilt of thyself be cast off.

17 And now it came to pass that these were the last words which the angel spake unto Alma, and he departed.

18 And now Alma and those that were with him fell again to the earth, for great was their astonishment; for with their own eyes they had beheld an angel of the Lord; and his voice was as thunder, which shook the earth; and they knew that there was nothing save the power of God that could shake the earth and cause it to tremble as though it would part asunder.

19 And now the astonishment of Alma was so great that he became dumb, that he could not open his mouth; yea, and he became weak, even that he could not move his hands; therefore he was taken by those that were with him, and carried helpless, even until he was laid before his father.

20 And they rehearsed unto his father all that had happened unto them; and his father rejoiced, for he knew that it was the power of God.

21 And he caused that a multitude should be gathered together that they might witness what the Lord had done for his son, and also for those that were with him.

22 And he caused that the priests should assemble themselves together; and they began to fast, and to pray to the Lord their God that he would

Date _____

☐ Completed

Date _____

☐ Completed

open the mouth of Alma, that he might speak, and also that his limbs might receive their strength—that the eyes of the people might be opened to see and know of the goodness and glory of God.

23 And it came to pass after they had fasted and prayed for the space of two days and two nights, the limbs of Alma received their strength, and he stood up and began to speak unto them, bidding them to be of good comfort:

24 For, said he, I have repented of my sins, and have been redeemed of the Lord; behold I am born of the Spirit.

25 And the Lord said unto me: Marvel not that all mankind, yea, men and women, all nations, kindreds, tongues and people, must be born again; yea, born of God, changed from their carnal and fallen state, to a state of righteousness, being redeemed of God, becoming his sons and daughters;

26 And thus they become new creatures; and unless they do this, they can in nowise inherit the kingdom of God.

27 I say unto you, unless this be the case, they must be cast off; and this I know, because I was like to be cast off.

28 Nevertheless, after wading through much tribulation, repenting nigh unto death, the Lord in mercy hath seen fit to snatch me out of an everlasting burning, and I am born of God.

29 My soul hath been redeemed from the gall of bitterness and bonds of iniquity. I was in the darkest abyss; but now I behold the marvelous light of God. My soul was racked with eternal torment; but I am snatched, and my soul is pained no more.

30 I rejected my Redeemer, and denied that which had been spoken of by our fathers; but now that they may foresee that he will come, and that he remembereth every creature of his creating, he will make himself manifest unto all.

31 Yea, every knee shall bow, and every tongue confess before him. Yea, even at the last day, when all men shall stand to be judged of him, then shall they confess that he is God; then shall they confess, who live without God in the world, that the judgment of an everlasting punishment is just upon them; and they shall quake, and tremble, and shrink beneath the glance of his all-searching eye.

32 And now it came to pass that Alma began from this time forward to teach the people, and those who were with Alma at the time the angel appeared unto them, traveling round about through all the land, publishing to all the people the things which they had heard and seen, and preaching the word of God in much tribulation, being greatly persecuted by those who were unbelievers, being smitten by many of them.

33 But notwithstanding all this, they did impart much consolation to the

Date _____
☐ Completed

Date _____
☐ Completed

church, confirming their faith, and exhorting them with long-suffering and much travail to keep the commandments of God.

34 And four of them were the sons of Mosiah; and their names were Ammon, and Aaron, and Omner, and Himni; these were the names of the sons of Mosiah.

35 And they traveled throughout all the land of Zarahemla, and among all the people who were under the reign of king Mosiah, zealously striving to repair all the injuries which they had done to the church, confessing all their sins, and publishing all the things which they had seen, and explaining the prophecies and the scriptures to all who desired to hear them.

36 And thus they were instruments in the hands of God in bringing many to the knowledge of the truth, yea, to the knowledge of their Redeemer.

37 And how blessed are they! For they did publish peace; they did publish good tidings of good; and they did declare unto the people that the Lord reigneth.

Date _____

☐ Completed

Mosiah

Chapter 28

Sight (Memorization) Words

word	work

Word Pattern or Rule

Pattern or Rule	-oo
Pattern words in scriptures	(none)
Location in chapter	(none)
Other words made from this patterns not found in chapter	bloom, boom, boost, boot, broom, choose, cool, coop, doom, food, fool, gloom, goof, groom, hoot, loom, loop, moo, mood, moon, noon, pool, proof, roof, room, roost, root, school, scoop, scoot, shoot, smooth, snoop, soon, spool, spoon, stool, too, tool, toot, troop, whoop, zoo

Phonics Application

- *Rule:* "W before OR, the OR makes the ER sound (work, word)" (Christian Center School Web site)*.
- *Complex Long Vowel Sounds:* long vowels make the sound of their name, but these complex long vowels do not contain the letter of the sound they are making. For example, "vein" makes the long A sound, but the vowels that combine to make the long A sound are "ei."
  - Long U—*oo*

Recommended (Age Appropriate) Reading Chunks

- Verses 1–4
- Verses 5–11
- Verses 12–16
- Verses 17–20

Gospel Principle Review/Activity

- How did Alma the Younger and the Sons of Mosiah change?
- Why did Alma the Younger and the Sons of Mosiah want to go to the Lamanites? Why was King Mosiah worried to send them?
- How did King Mosiah translate the brass plates?
- *Activity:* What does the device look like that King Mosiah used to translate the plates? Look at verse 13 and build a replica of the translator.

Word Patterns

oo ___

Words made with –oo word pattern.
Use alphabet letters to create words.

Mosiah 28

1 Now it came to pass that after the sons of Mosiah had done all these things, they took a small number with them and returned to their father, the king, and desired of him that he would grant unto them that they might, with these whom they had selected, go up to the land of Nephi that they might preach the things which they had heard, and that they might impart the word of God to their brethren, the Lamanites—

2 That perhaps they might bring them to the knowledge of the Lord their God, and convince them of the iniquity of their fathers; and that perhaps they might cure them of their hatred towards the Nephites, that they might also be brought to rejoice in the Lord their God, that they might become friendly to one another, and that there should be no more contentions in all the land which the Lord their God had given them.

3 Now they were desirous that salvation should be declared to every creature, for they could not bear that any human soul should perish; yea, even the very thoughts that any soul should endure endless torment did cause them to quake and tremble.

4 And thus did the Spirit of the Lord work upon them, for they were the very vilest of sinners. And the Lord saw fit in his infinite mercy to spare them; nevertheless they suffered much anguish of soul because of their iniquities, suffering much and fearing that they should be cast off forever.

Date _____
☐ Completed

5 And it came to pass that they did plead with their father many days that they might go up to the land of Nephi.

6 And king Mosiah went and inquired of the Lord if he should let his sons go up among the Lamanites to preach the word.

7 And the Lord said unto Mosiah: Let them go up, for many shall believe on their words, and they shall have eternal life; and I will deliver people sons out of the hands of the Lamanites.

8 And it came to pass that Mosiah granted that they might go and do according to their request.

9 And they took their journey into the wilderness to go up to preach the word among the Lamanites; and I shall give an account of their proceedings hereafter.

10 Now king Mosiah had no one to confer the kingdom upon, for there was not any of his sons who would accept of the kingdom.

11 Therefore he took the records which were engraven on the plates of brass, and also the plates of Nephi, and all the things which he had kept and preserved according to the commandments of God, after having translated and caused to be written the records which were on the plates of gold which had been found by the people of Limhi, which were delivered to him by the hand of Limhi;

Date _____
☐ Completed

12 And this he did because of the great anxiety of his people; for they were desirous beyond measure to know concerning those people who had been destroyed.

13 And now he translated them by the means of those two stones which were fastened into the two rims of a bow.

14 Now these things were prepared from the beginning, and were handed down from generation to generation, for the purpose of interpreting languages;

15 And they have been kept and preserved by the hand of the Lord, that he should discover to every creature who should possess the land the iniquities and abominations of his people;

16 And whosoever has these things is called seer, after the manner of old times.

---

17 Now after Mosiah had finished translating these records, behold, it gave an account of the people who were destroyed, from the time that they were destroyed back to the building of the great tower, at the time the Lord confounded the language of the people and they were scattered abroad upon the face of all the earth, yea, and even from that time back until the creation of Adam.

18 Now this account did cause the people of Mosiah to mourn exceedingly, yea, they were filled with sorrow; nevertheless it gave them much knowledge, in the which they did rejoice.

19 And this account shall be written hereafter; for behold, it is expedient that all people should know the things which are written in this account.

20 And now, as I said unto you, that after king Mosiah had done these things, he took the plates of brass, and all the things which he had kept, and conferred them upon Alma, who was the son of Alma; yea, all the records, and also the interpreters, and conferred them upon him, and commanded him that he should keep and preserve them, and also keep a record of the people, handing them down from one generation to another, even as they had been handed down from the time that Lehi left Jerusalem.

Date _____
☐ Completed

Date _____
☐ Completed

Mosiah

Chapter 29—Review

Sight (Memorization) Words

love	was	body	heart	began	word	work

Phonics Application

- *Complex Long Vowel Sounds:* long vowels make the sound of their name, but these complex long vowels do not contain the letter of the sound they are making. For example, "vein" makes the long A sound, but the vowels that combine to make the long A sound are "ei."
  - Long A (ei, ey)
  - Long I (y/ye, igh)
  - Long O (ow)
  - Long U (oo)

Recommended (Age Appropriate) Reading Chunks

- Verses 1–6
- Verses 7–12
- Verses 13–18
- Verses 19–23
- Verses 24–30
- Verses 31–35
- Verses 36–40
- Verses 41–47

Gospel Principle Review/Activity

- Why does Mosiah suggest that they should change their government to judges?
- Why don't King Mosiah's sons want to be king?
- *Activity:* This is the end of volume 2, and we just changed from having a king be the ruler to many judges ruling the people.
  - Record in your journal your predictions (or guesses) about what will happen with the judges ruling the people, instead of a king.
  - Record in your journal how your feel about the Book of Mormon. Is reading the Book of Mormon getting easier for you?

Word Patterns—Review

Find the words in the word box in the word search.

E	W	R	Z	J	J	M	V	Q	G
T	D	C	I	O	M	N	U	G	S
H	J	B	Z	G	U	M	Y	D	M
E	G	N	F	B	H	G	E	E	M
Y	R	C	K	L	H	T	Q	A	L
C	G	N	R	T	C	K	U	A	S
E	O	E	O	E	I	G	H	T	D
W	R	O	V	A	U	Z	V	J	X
J	M	S	Q	L	A	J	J	P	W
S	A	T	N	B	V	N	X	D	J

Word Box

cry

eight

know

right

smooth

they

Mosiah 29

1 Now when Mosiah had done this he sent out throughout all the land, among all the people, desiring to know their will concerning who should be their king.

2 And it came to pass that the voice of the people came, saying: We are desirous that Aaron people son should be our king and our ruler.

3 Now Aaron had gone up to the land of Nephi, therefore the king could not confer the kingdom upon him; neither would Aaron take upon him the kingdom; neither were any of the sons of Mosiah willing to take upon them the kingdom.

4 Therefore king Mosiah sent again among the people; yea, even a written word sent he among the people. And these were the words that were written, saying:

5 Behold, O ye my people, or my brethren, for I esteem you as such, I desire that ye should consider the cause which ye are called to consider—for ye are desirous to have a king.

6 Now I declare unto you that he to whom the kingdom doth rightly belong has declined, and will not take upon him the kingdom.

Date _____
☐ Completed

7 And now if there should be another appointed in his stead, behold I fear there would rise contentions among you. And who knoweth but what my son, to whom the kingdom doth belong, should turn to be angry and draw away a part of this people after him, which would cause wars and contentions among you, which would be the cause of shedding much blood and perverting the way of the Lord, yea, and destroy the souls of many people.

8 Now I say unto you let us be wise and consider these things, for we have no right to destroy my son, neither should we have any right to destroy another if he should be appointed in his stead.

9 And if my son should turn again to his pride and vain things he would recall the things which he had said, and claim his right to the kingdom, which would cause him and also this people to commit much sin.

10 And now let us be wise and look forward to these things, and do that which will make for the peace of this people.

11 Therefore I will be your king the remainder of my days; nevertheless, let us appoint judges, to judge this people according to our law; and we will newly arrange the affairs of this people, for we will appoint wise men to be judges, that will judge this people according to the commandments of God.

12 Now it is better that a man should be judged of God than of man, for the judgments of God are always just, but the judgments of man are not always just.

Date _____
☐ Completed

13 Therefore, if it were possible that you could have just men to be your kings, who would establish the laws of God, and judge this people according to his commandments, yea, if ye could have men for your kings who would do even as my father Benjamin did for this people—I say unto you, if this could always be the case then it would be expedient that ye should always have kings to rule over you.

14 And even I myself have labored with all the power and faculties which I have possessed, to teach you the commandments of God, and to establish peace throughout the land, that there should be no wars nor contentions, no stealing, nor plundering, nor murdering, nor any manner of iniquity;

15 And whosoever has committed iniquity, him have I punished according to the crime which he has committed, according to the law which has been given to us by our fathers.

16 Now I say unto you, that because all men are not just it is not expedient that ye should have a king or kings to rule over you.

17 For behold, how much iniquity doth one wicked king cause to be committed, yea, and what great destruction!

18 Yea, remember king Noah, his wickedness and his abominations, and also the wickedness and abominations of his people. Behold what great destruction did come upon them; and also because of their iniquities they were brought into bondage.

19 And were it not for the interposition of their all-wise Creator, and this because of their sincere repentance, they must unavoidably remain in bondage until now.

20 But behold, he did deliver them because they did humble themselves before him; and because they cried mightily unto him he did deliver them out of bondage; and thus doth the Lord work with his power in all cases among the children of men, extending the arm of mercy towards them that put their trust in him.

21 And behold, now I say unto you, ye cannot dethrone an iniquitous king save it be through much contention, and the shedding of much blood.

22 For behold, he has his friends in iniquity, and he keepeth his guards about him; and he teareth up the laws of those who have reigned in righteousness before him; and he trampleth under his feet the commandments of God;

23 And he enacteth laws, and sendeth them forth among his people, yea, laws after the manner of his own wickedness; and whosoever doth not obey his laws he causeth to be destroyed; and whosoever doth rebel against him he will send his armies against them to war, and if he can he will destroy them; and thus an unrighteous king doth pervert the ways of all righteousness.

Date _____
☐ Completed

Date _____
☐ Completed

24 And now behold I say unto you, it is not expedient that such abominations should come upon you.

25 Therefore, choose you by the voice of this people, judges, that ye may be judged according to the laws which have been given you by our fathers, which are correct, and which were given them by the hand of the Lord.

26 Now it is not common that the voice of the people desireth anything contrary to that which is right; but it is common for the lesser part of the people to desire that which is not right; therefore this shall ye observe and make it your law—to do your business by the voice of the people.

27 And if the time comes that the voice of the people doth choose iniquity, then is the time that the judgments of God will come upon you; yea, then is the time he will visit you with great destruction even as he has hitherto visited this land.

28 And now if ye have judges, and they do not judge you according to the law which has been given, ye can cause that they may be judged of a higher judge.

29 If your higher judges do not judge righteous judgments, ye shall cause that a small number of your lower judges should be gathered together, and they shall judge your higher judges, according to the voice of the people.

30 And I command you to do these things in the fear of the Lord; and I command you to do these things, and that ye have no king; that if these people commit sins and iniquities they shall be answered upon their own heads.

31 For behold I say unto you, the sins of many people have been caused by the iniquities of their kings; therefore their iniquities are answered upon the heads of their kings.

32 And now I desire that this inequality should be no more in this land, especially among this my people; but I desire that this land be a land of liberty, and every man may enjoy his rights and privileges alike, so long as the Lord sees fit that we may live and inherit the land, yea, even as long as any of our posterity remains upon the face of the land.

33 And many more things did king Mosiah write unto them, unfolding unto them all the trials and troubles of a righteous king, yea, all the travails of soul for their people, and also all the murmurings of the people to their king; and he explained it all unto them.

34 And he told them that these things ought not to be; but that the burden should come upon all the people, that every man might bear his part.

35 And he also unfolded unto them all the disadvantages they labored under, by having an unrighteous king to rule over them;

36 Yea, all his iniquities and abominations, and all the wars, and contentions, and bloodshed, and the stealing, and the plundering, and the

committing of whoredoms, and all manner of iniquities which cannot be enumerated—telling them that these things ought not to be, that they were expressly repugnant to the commandments of God.

37 And now it came to pass, after king Mosiah had sent these things forth among the people they were convinced of the truth of his words.

38 Therefore they relinquished their desires for a king, and became exceedingly anxious that every man should have an equal chance throughout all the land; yea, and every man expressed a willingness to answer for his own sins.

39 Therefore, it came to pass that they assembled themselves together in bodies throughout the land, to cast in their voices concerning who should be their judges, to judge them according to the law which had been given them; and they were exceedingly rejoiced because of the liberty which had been granted unto them.

40 And they did wax strong in love towards Mosiah; yea, they did esteem him more than any other man; for they did not look upon him as a tyrant who was seeking for gain, yea, for that lucre which doth corrupt the soul; for he had not exacted riches of them, neither had he delighted in the shedding of blood; but he had established peace in the land, and he had granted unto his people that they should be delivered from all manner of bondage; therefore they did esteem him, yea, exceedingly, beyond measure.

41 And it came to pass that they did appoint judges to rule over them, or to judge them according to the law; and this they did throughout all the land.

42 And it came to pass that Alma was appointed to be the first chief judge, he being also the high priest, his father having conferred the office upon him, and having given him the charge concerning all the affairs of the church.

43 And now it came to pass that Alma did walk in the ways of the Lord, and he did keep his commandments, and he did judge righteous judgments; and there was continual peace through the land.

44 And thus commenced the reign of the judges throughout all the land of Zarahemla, among all the people who were called the Nephites; and Alma was the first and chief judge.

45 And now it came to pass that his father died, being eighty and two years old, having lived to fulfil the commandments of God.

46 And it came to pass that Mosiah died also, in the thirty and third year of his reign, being sixty and three years old; making in the whole, five hundred and nine years from the time Lehi left Jerusalem.

47 And thus ended the reign of the kings over the people of Nephi; and thus ended the days of Alma, who was the founder of their church.

Date _____
☐ Completed

Date _____
☐ Completed

Endnotes

1. "Every Child Reading: Outreach Kit, Dyslexia: Characteristics and Effective Intervention." Baltimore, MD The International Dyslexia Association, 2005.
2. *LD Online.* Online. Accessed 2006; available from ldonline.org/.
3. Gordon B. Hinckley, "Forgiveness," *Ensign*, Nov. 2005, 81.

Sources Consulted

American Heritage Dictionary—Third Edition. New York, New York: Dell Publishing, 1994.

AVKO Educational Research Foundation. Online. "The Learning Disabilities/Dyslexia Specialists." Accessed February 15, 2005; available from www.speccling.org/Freebies/ie_rule.htm.

Bear, Donald R., Marcia Invernizzi, Shane Templeton, and Francine Johnston. *Words Their Way—Word Study for Phonics, Vocabulary, and Spelling Instruction, 2nd ed.* Columbus, Ohio: Merrill an imprint of Prentice Hall, 2000.

Beck, Isabel, L., Margaret G. McKeown, and Linda Kucan. *Bringing Words to Life, Robust Vocabulary Instruction.* New York, London: The Guilford Press, 2002.

Holy Bible, King James Version. Bible Dictionary. Salt Lake City: The Church of Jesus Christ of Latter-day Saints, 1981.

Book of Mormon. Index. Salt Lake City: The Church of Jesus Christ of Latter-day Saints,1981.

Cook, Vivian. Online. "I Before E Rule." *Writing Systems.* Accessed May 25, 2006; available from homepage. ntlworld.com/vivian.c/EnglishSpellingSystem/IbeforeE.htm.

Cunningham, Bob. Online. "Exceptions to the Rule 'I before E Except After C.'" Accessed February 23, 2002; available from alt-usage-english.org/I_before_E.html.

Doyle, Dennis. Online. "Phonics, Syllable and Accent Rules." Accessed May 25, 2006; available from english. glendale.cc.ca.us/phonics.rules.html.